Monster Science

ZOMBIES
AND FORCES AND MOTION

BY MARK WEAKLAND • ILLUSTRATED BY GERVASIO

Consultant:
Joanne K. Olson, PhD
Associate Professor, Science Education
Iowa State University
Ames, Iowa

IN MEMORY OF THOMAS

CAPSTONE PRESS
a capstone imprint

Graphic Library is published by Capstone Press,
151 Good Counsel Drive, P.O. Box 669, Mankato, Minnesota 56002.
www.capstonepub.com

Books published by Capstone Press are manufactured with paper
containing at least 10 percent post-consumer waste.

Library of Congress Cataloging-in-Publication Data
Weakland, Mark.
  Zombies and forces and motion / by Mark Weakland ; illustrated by Gervasio.
    p. cm.—(Graphic library. Monster science)
  Summary: "In cartoon format, uses zombies to explain the science of forces and motion"—
Provided by publisher.
  Includes bibliographical references and index.
  ISBN 978-1-4296-6577-3 (library binding)
  ISBN 978-1-4296-7335-8 (paperback)
  1. Force and energy—Juvenile literature. 2. Motion—Juvenile literature. I. Gervasio, ill.
II. Title.
  QC73.4.W43 2012
  531'.6—dc22
                                                                            2011001018

Editor
Christopher L. Harbo

Art Director
Nathan Gassman

Designer
Lori Bye

Production Specialist
Eric Manske

Printed in the United States of America in Stevens Point, Wisconsin.
032011   006111WZF11

TABLE OF CONTENTS

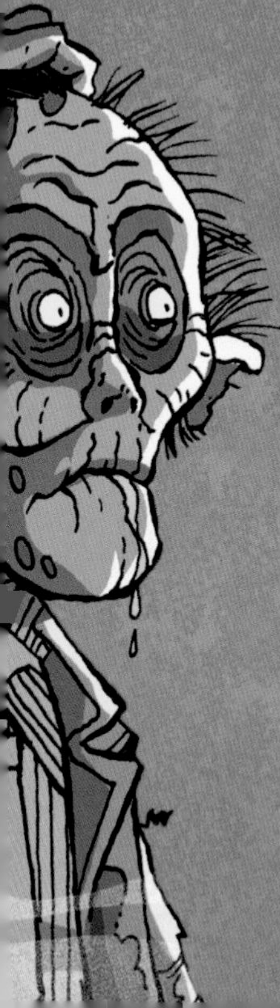

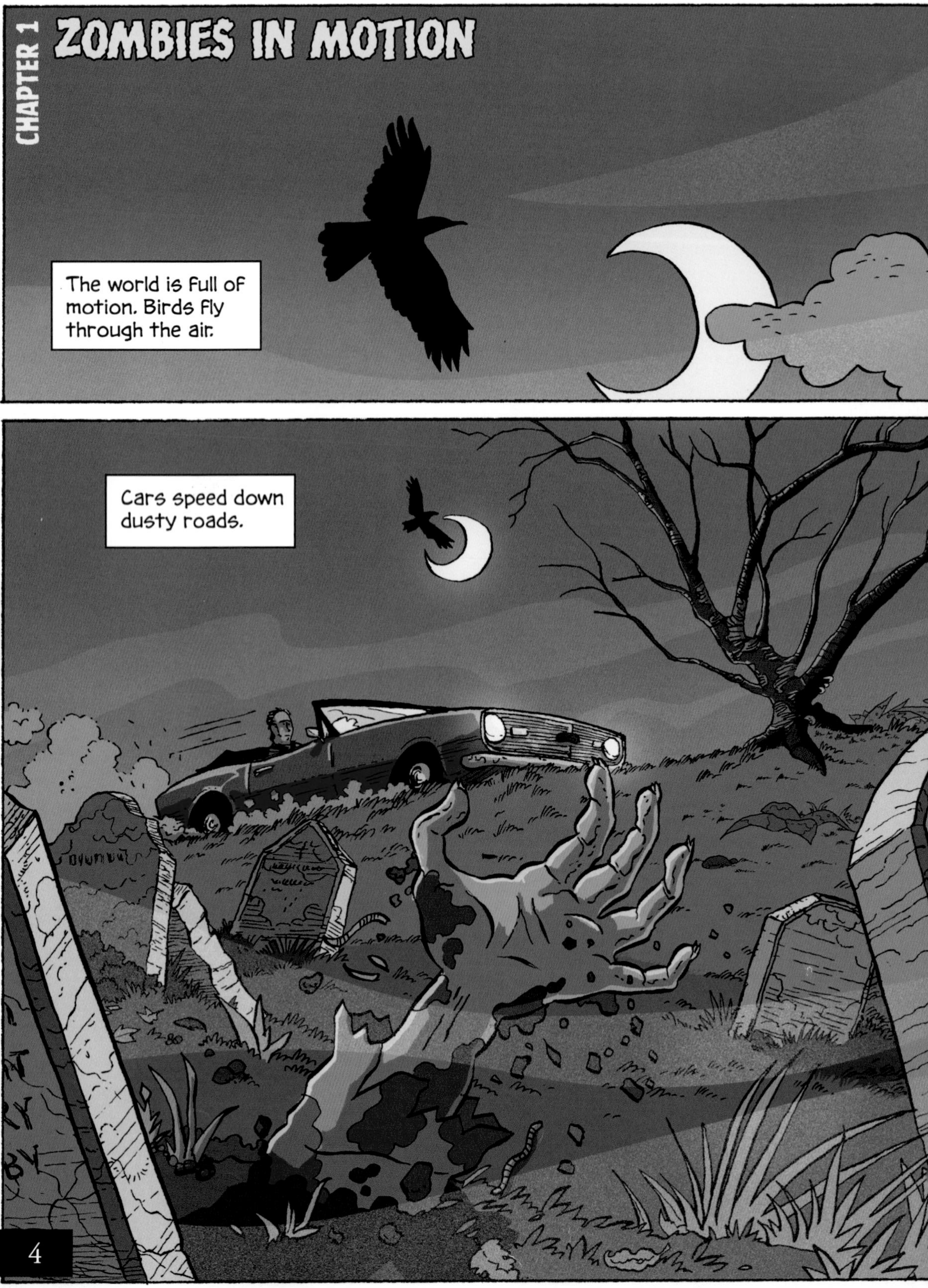
CHAPTER 1
ZOMBIES IN MOTION
The world is full of motion. Birds fly through the air.
Cars speed down dusty roads.

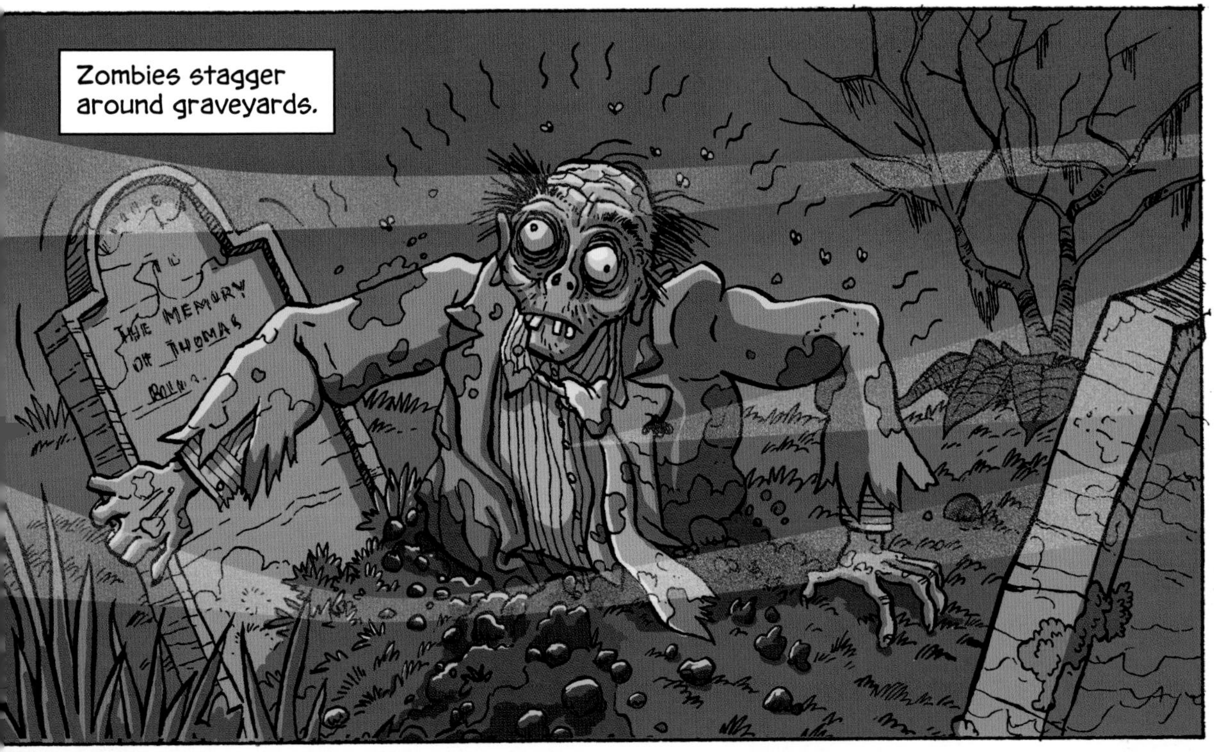
Zombies stagger around graveyards.
THE MEMORY
OF THOMAS

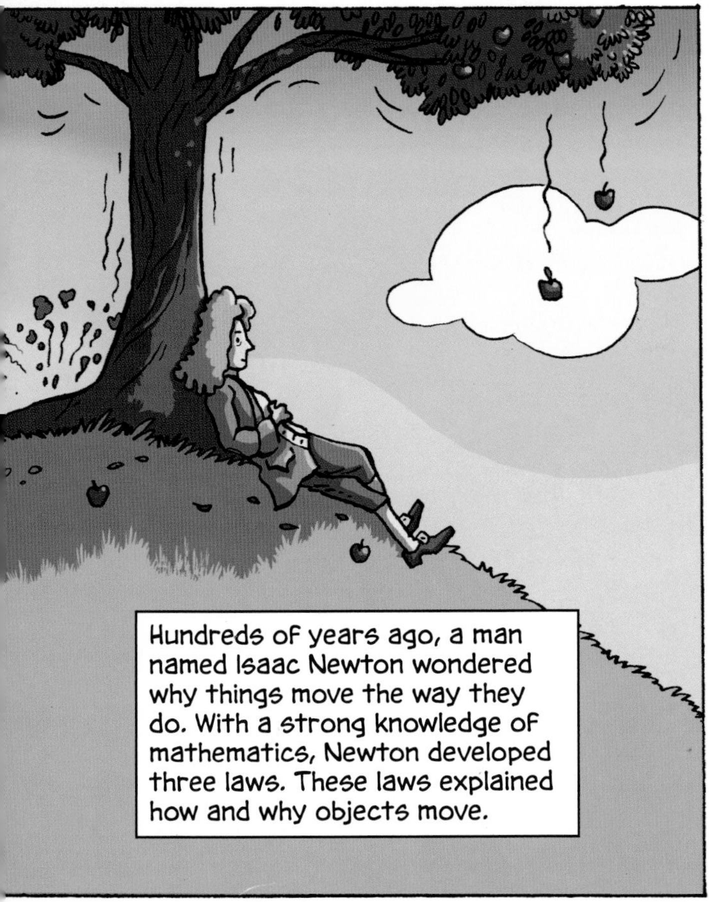
Hundreds of years ago, a man named Isaac Newton wondered why things move the way they do. With a strong knowledge of mathematics, Newton developed three laws. These laws explained how and why objects move.

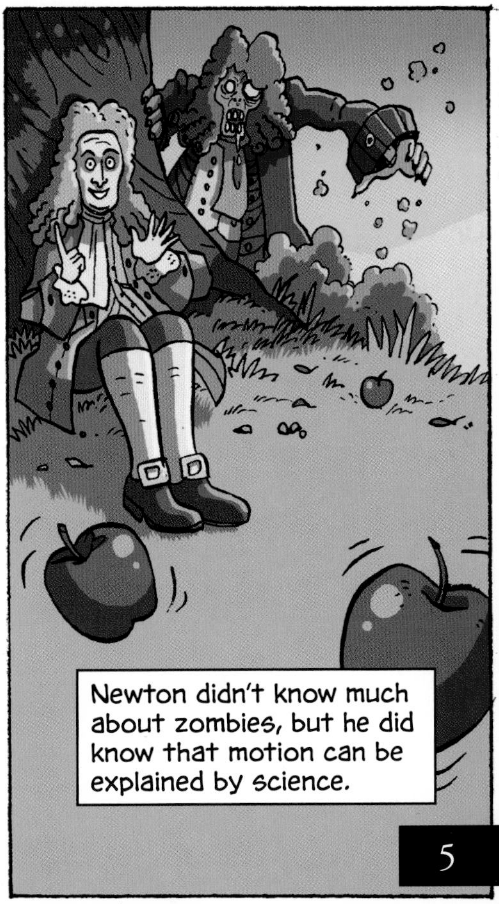
Newton didn't know much about zombies, but he did know that motion can be explained by science.

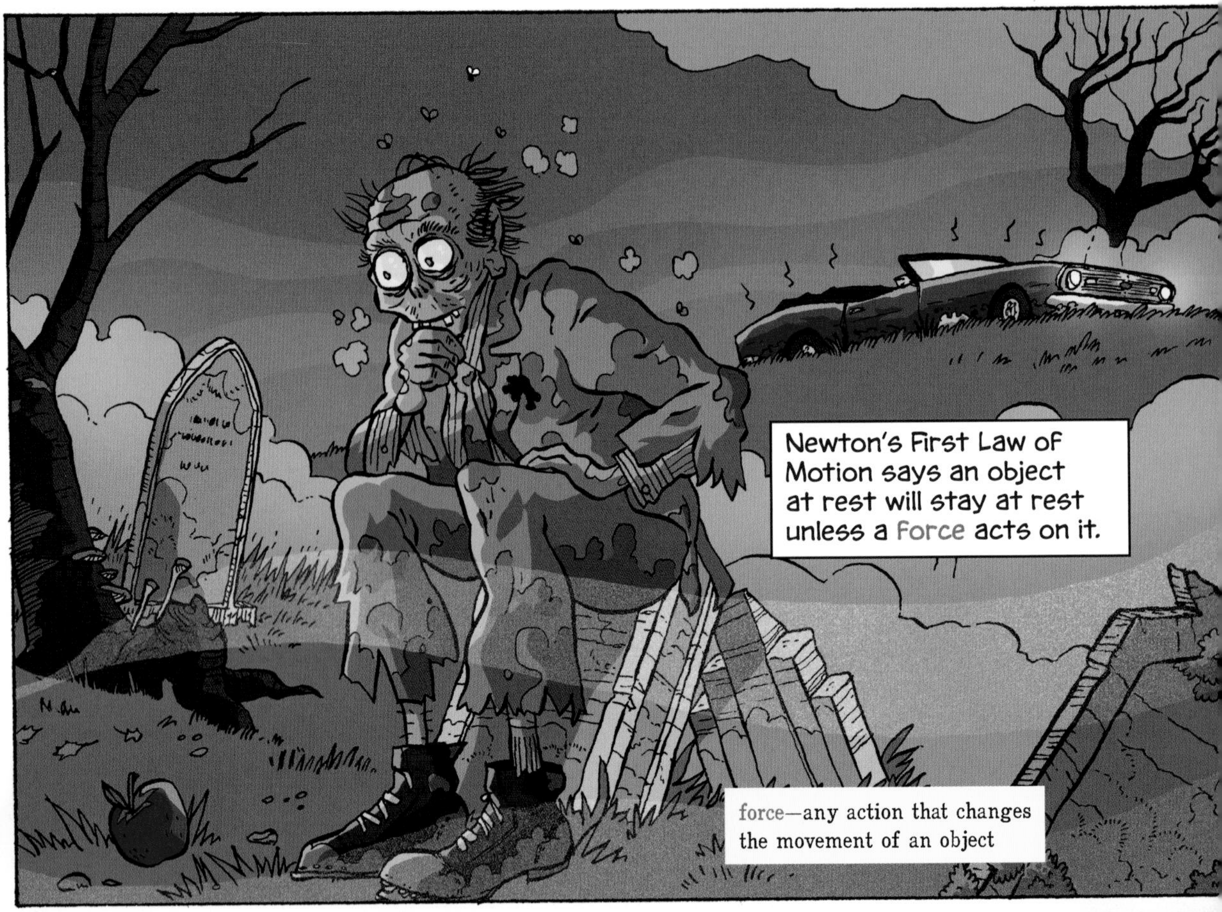
Newton's First Law of Motion says an object at rest will stay at rest unless a force acts on it.
force—any action that changes the movement of an object

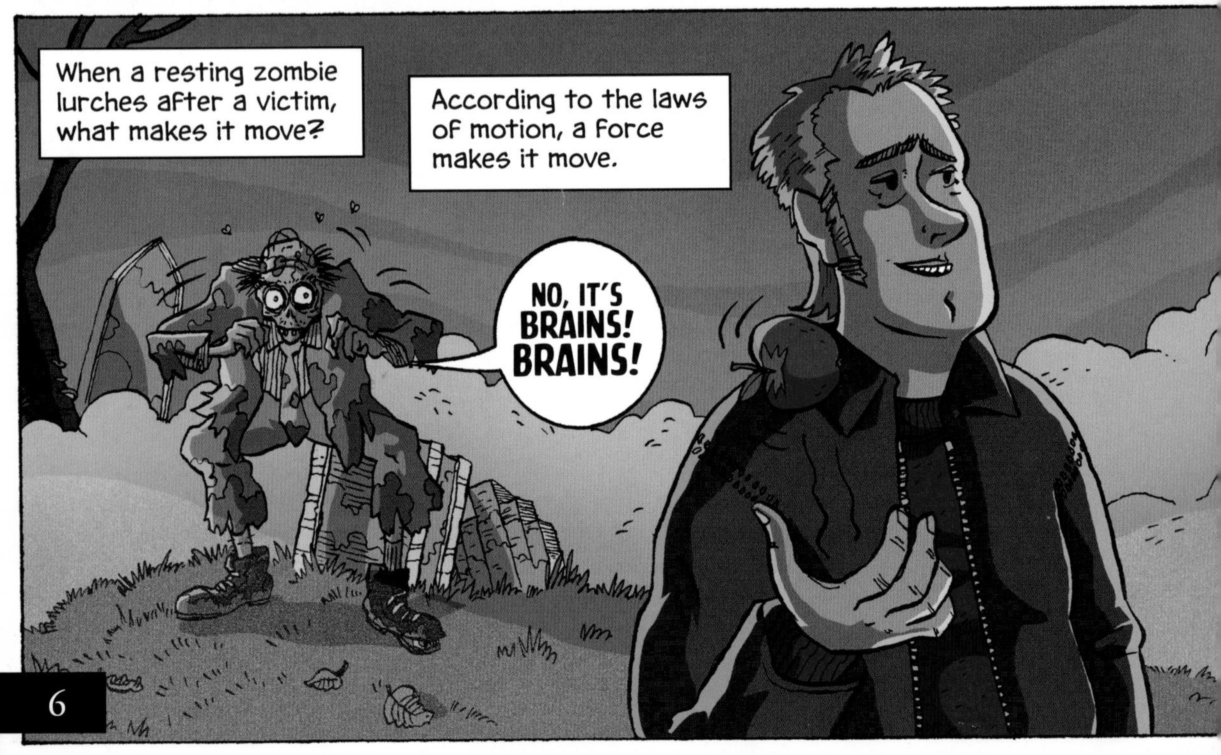
When a resting zombie lurches after a victim, what makes it move?
According to the laws of motion, a force makes it move.
NO, IT'S BRAINS! BRAINS!

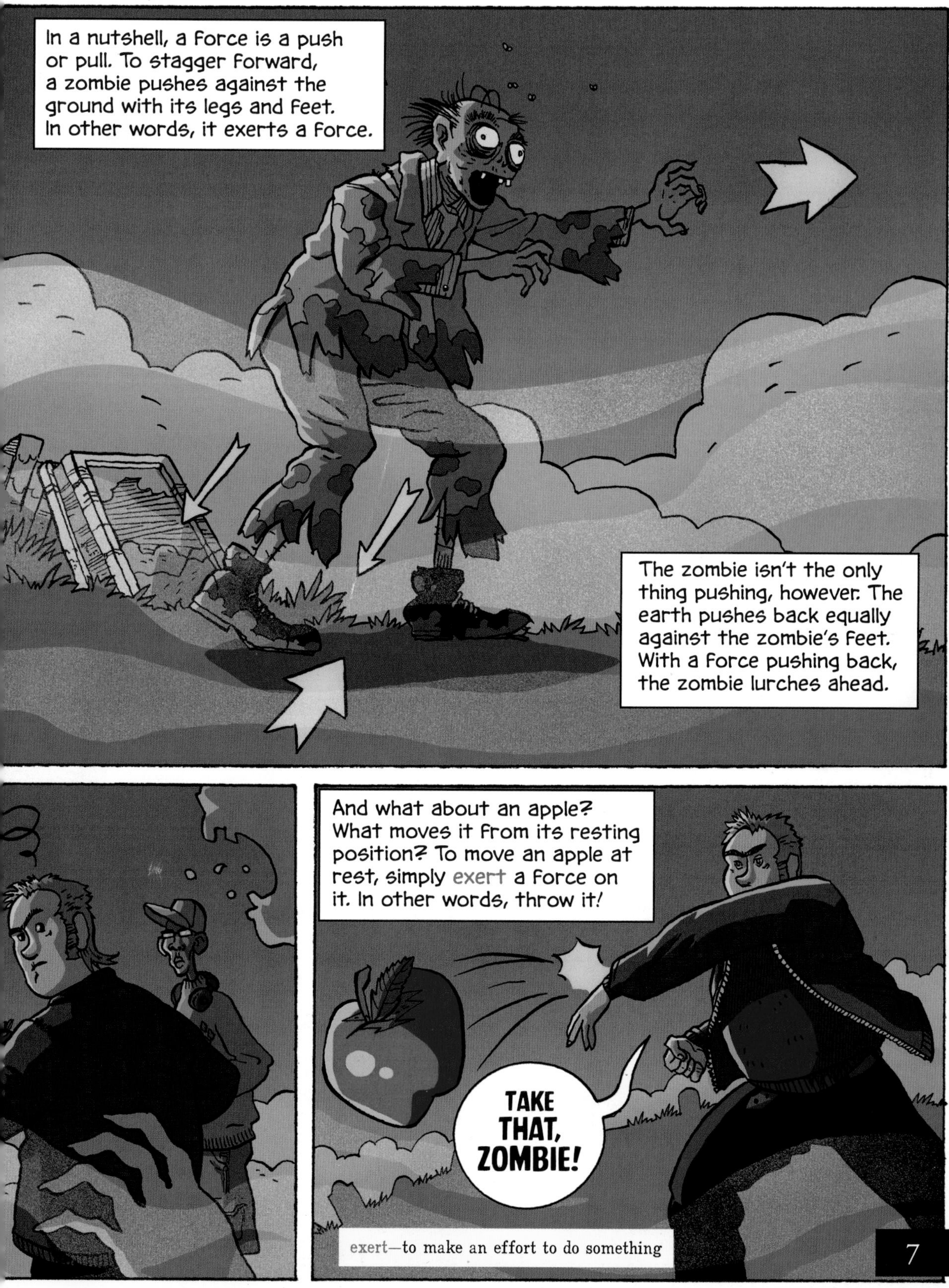
In a nutshell, a force is a push or pull. To stagger forward, a zombie pushes against the ground with its legs and feet. In other words, it exerts a force.
The zombie isn't the only thing pushing, however. The earth pushes back equally against the zombie's feet. With a force pushing back, the zombie lurches ahead.
And what about an apple? What moves it from its resting position? To move an apple at rest, simply exert a force on it. In other words, throw it!
TAKE THAT, ZOMBIE!

exert—to make an effort to do something

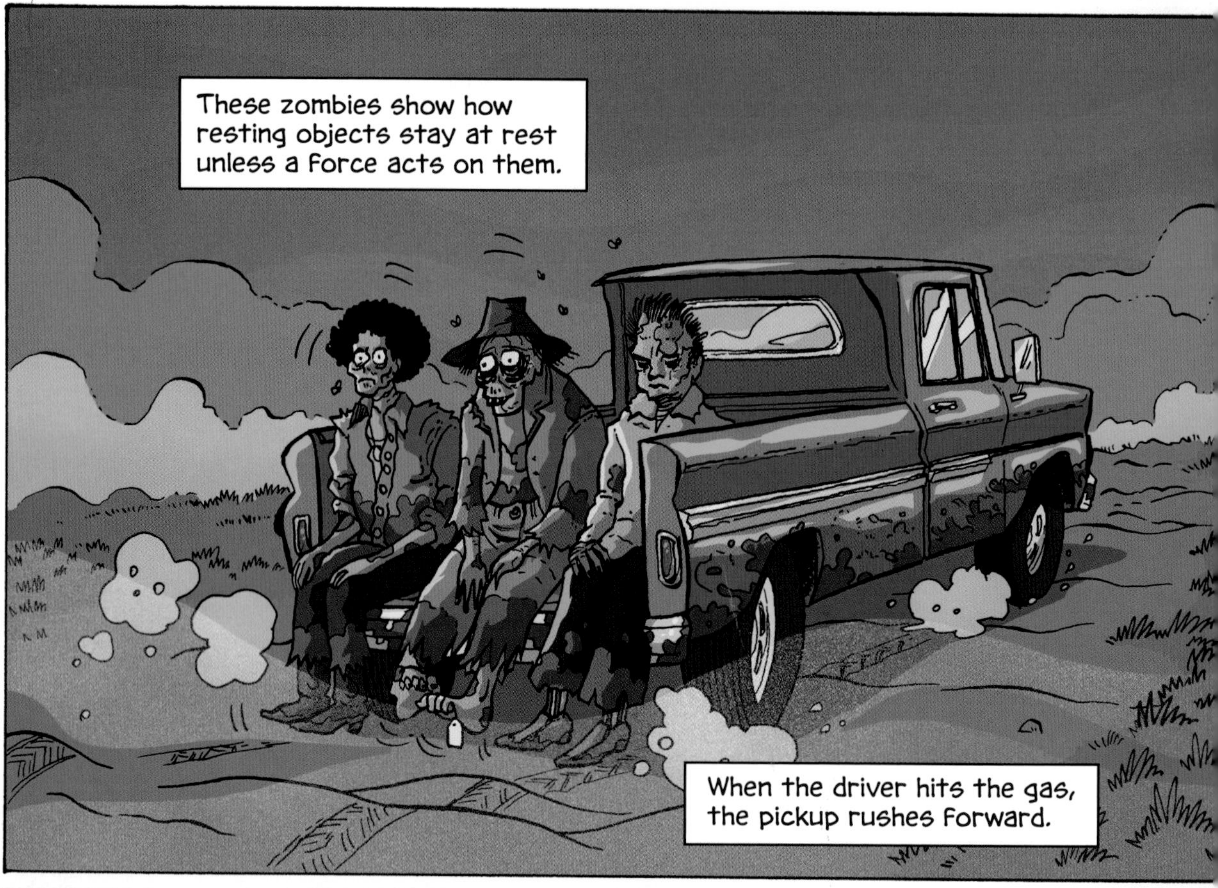
These zombies show how resting objects stay at rest unless a force acts on them.
When the driver hits the gas, the pickup rushes forward.

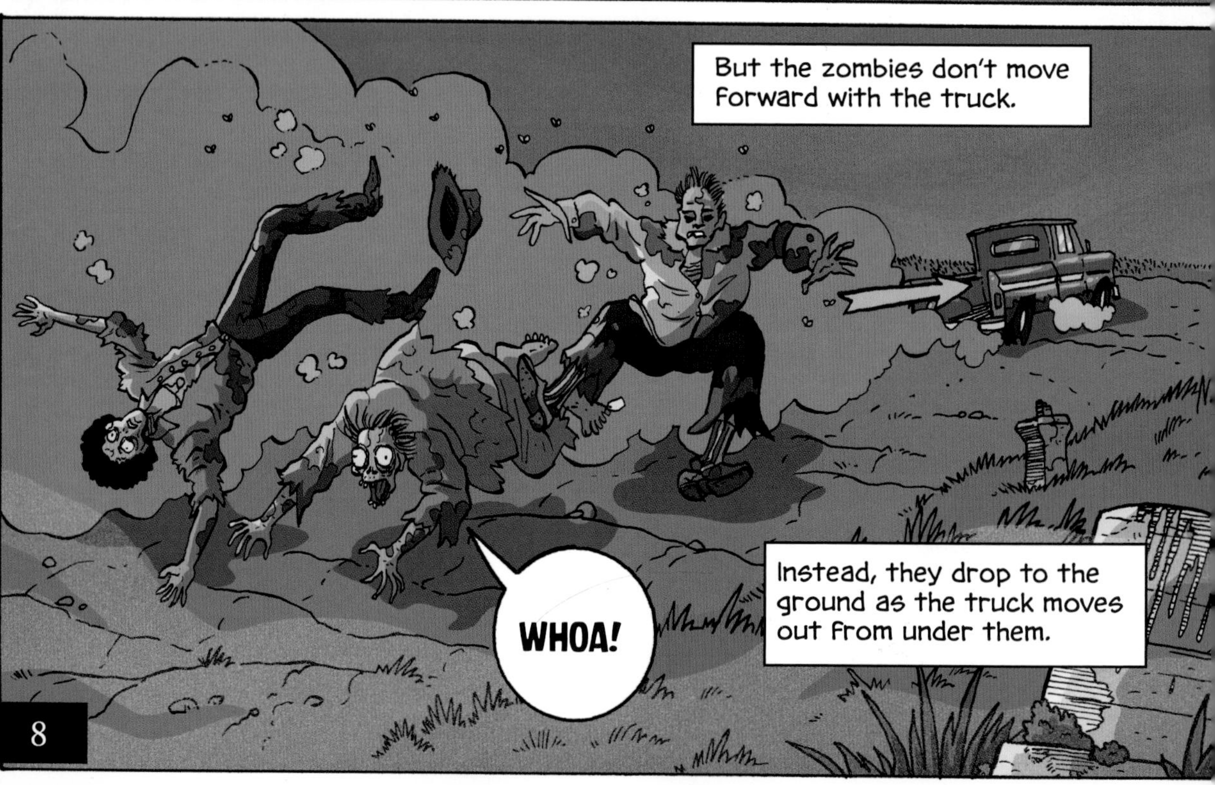
But the zombies don't move forward with the truck.
Instead, they drop to the ground as the truck moves out from under them.
WHOA!

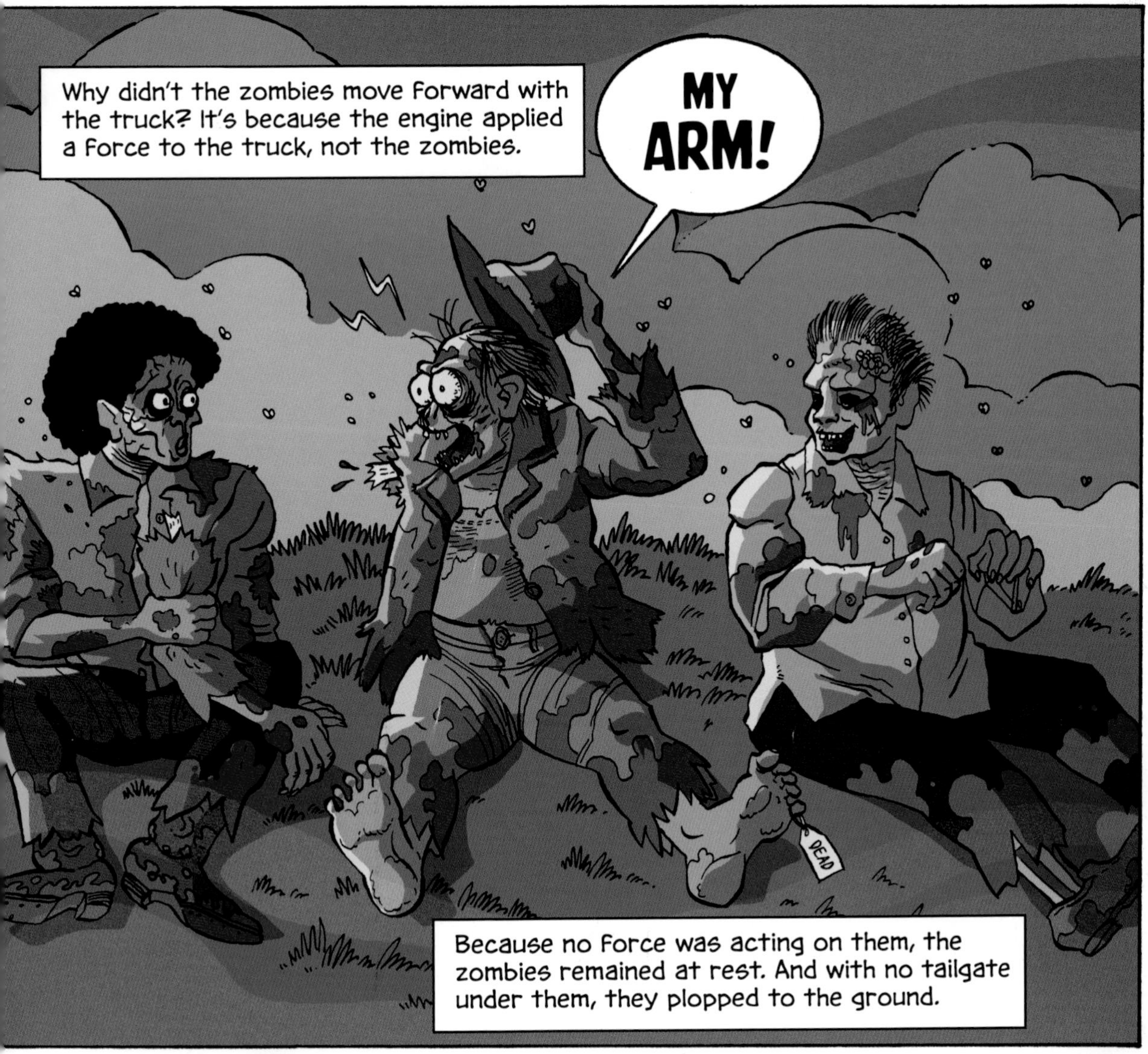
Why didn't the zombies move forward with the truck? It's because the engine applied a force to the truck, not the zombies.
MY ARM!
DEAD
Because no force was acting on them, the zombies remained at rest. And with no tailgate under them, they plopped to the ground.

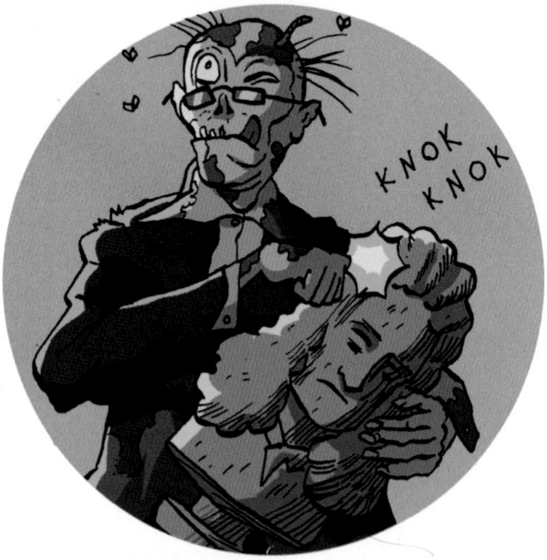
KNOK KNOK

ISAAC NEWTON

Isaac Newton gave us a much greater understanding of how the universe works. Using prisms he showed how white light is made up of many colors. He proposed that gravity is the force pulling on every object in the universe. Newton also figured out how our solar system's planets move along their paths.

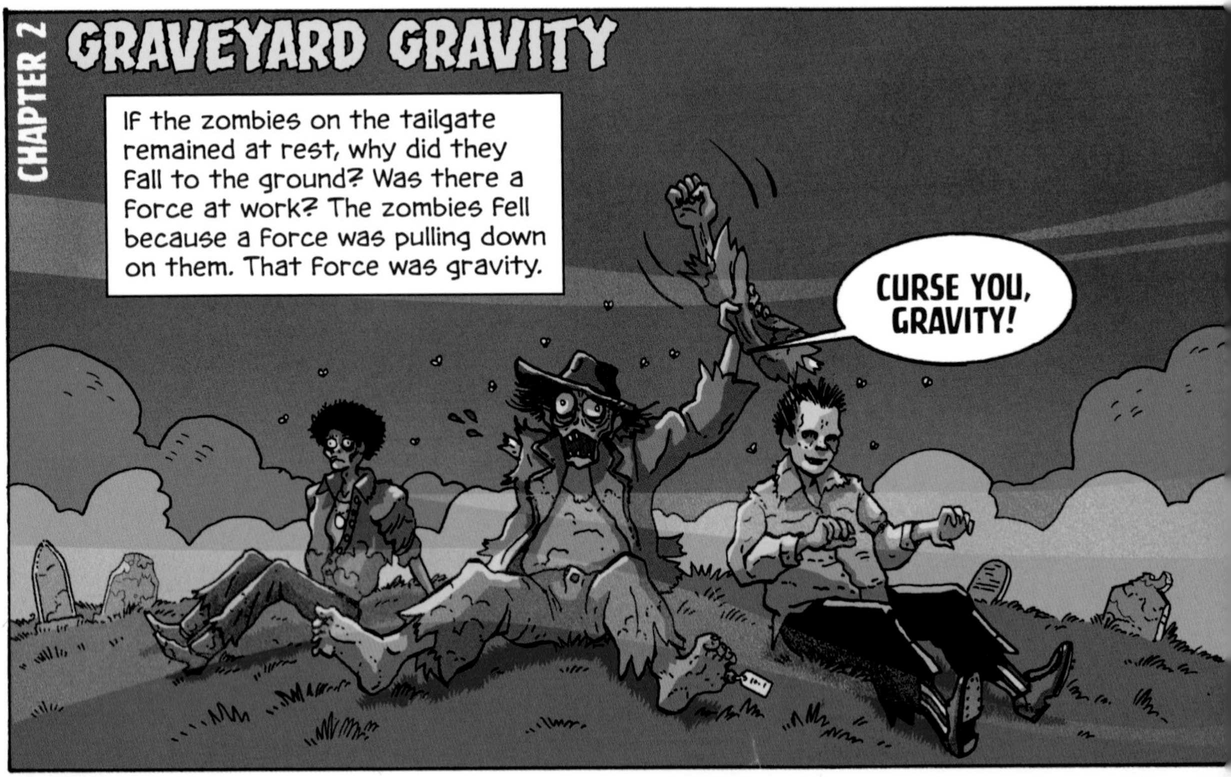
CHAPTER 2
GRAVEYARD GRAVITY
If the zombies on the tailgate remained at rest, why did they fall to the ground? Was there a force at work? The zombies fell because a force was pulling down on them. That force was gravity.
CURSE YOU, GRAVITY!

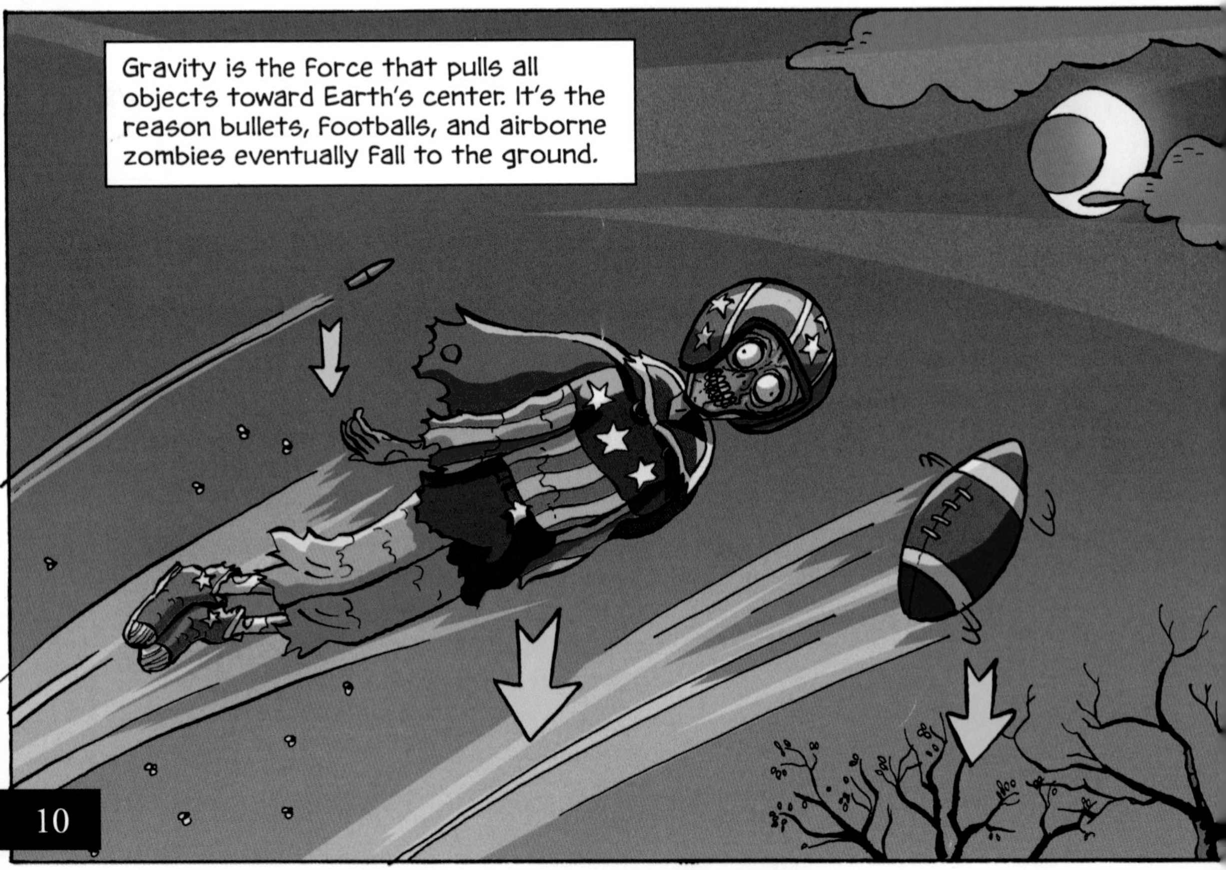
Gravity is the force that pulls all objects toward Earth's center. It's the reason bullets, footballs, and airborne zombies eventually fall to the ground.

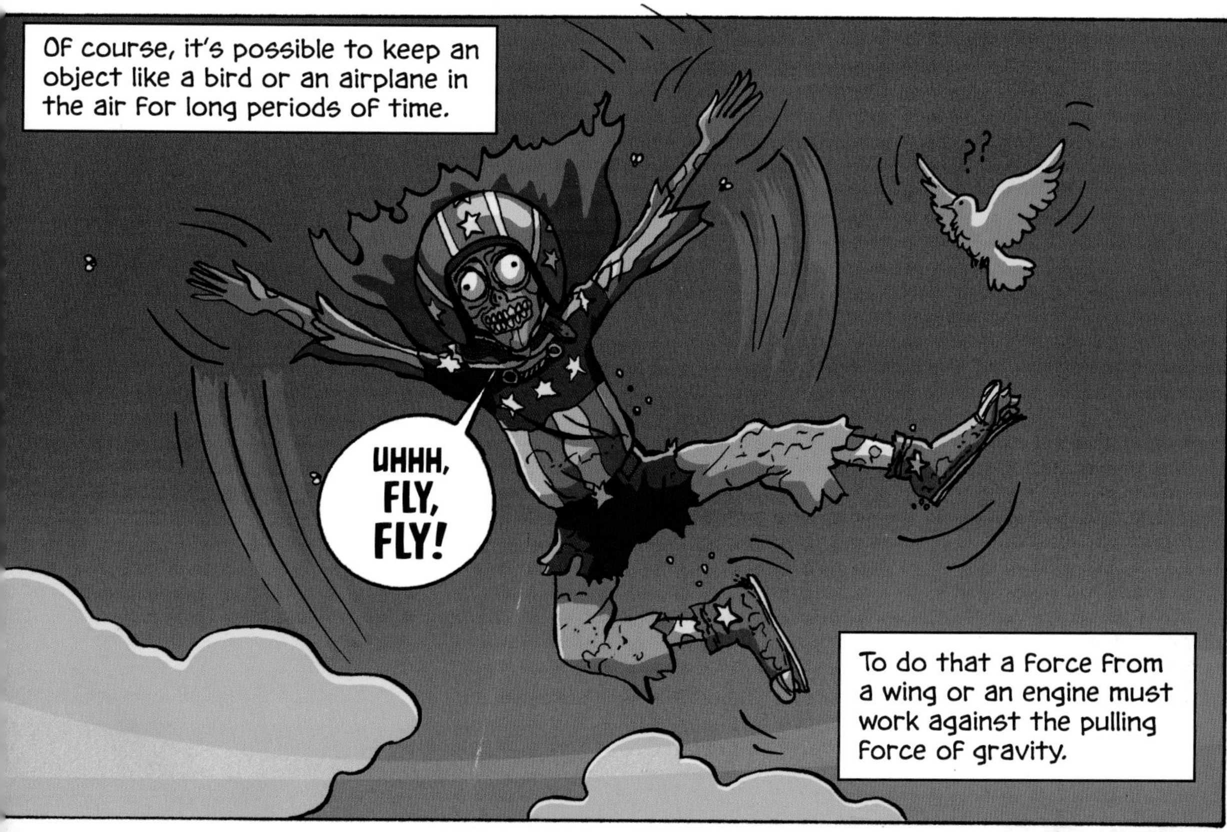
Of course, it's possible to keep an object like a bird or an airplane in the air for long periods of time.
??
UHHH, FLY, FLY!
To do that a force from a wing or an engine must work against the pulling force of gravity.

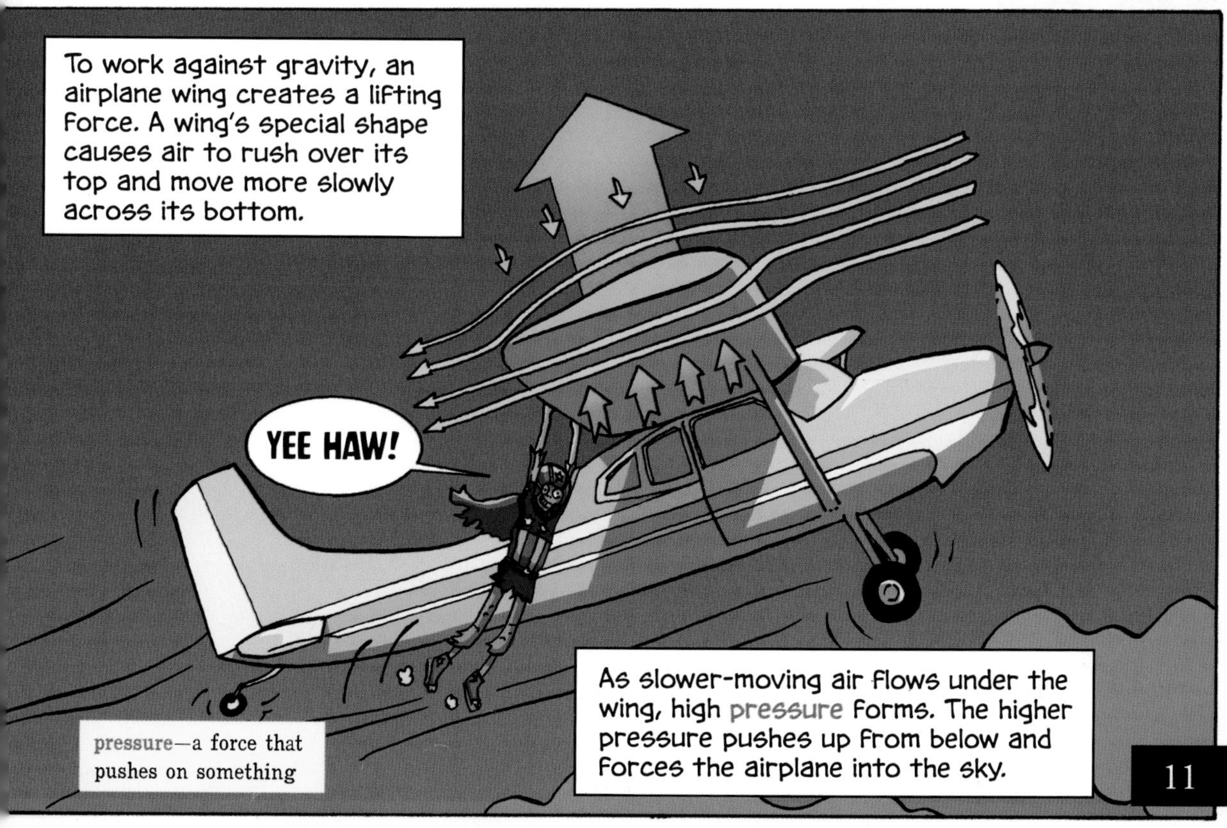
To work against gravity, an airplane wing creates a lifting force. A wing's special shape causes air to rush over its top and move more slowly across its bottom.
YEE HAW!
As slower-moving air flows under the wing, high pressure forms. The higher pressure pushes up from below and forces the airplane into the sky.

pressure—a force that pushes on something

CHAPTER 3

CHANGING A ZOMBIE'S DIRECTION

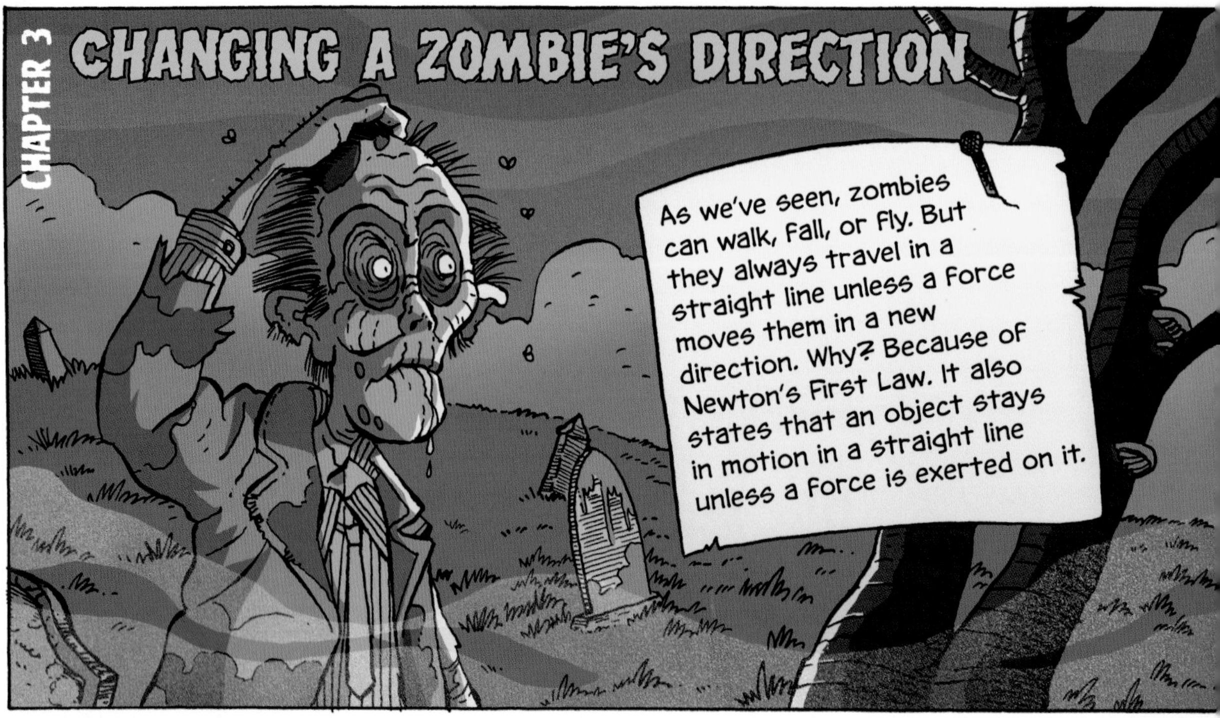
As we've seen, zombies can walk, fall, or fly. But they always travel in a straight line unless a force moves them in a new direction. Why? Because of Newton's First Law. It also states that an object stays in motion in a straight line unless a force is exerted on it.

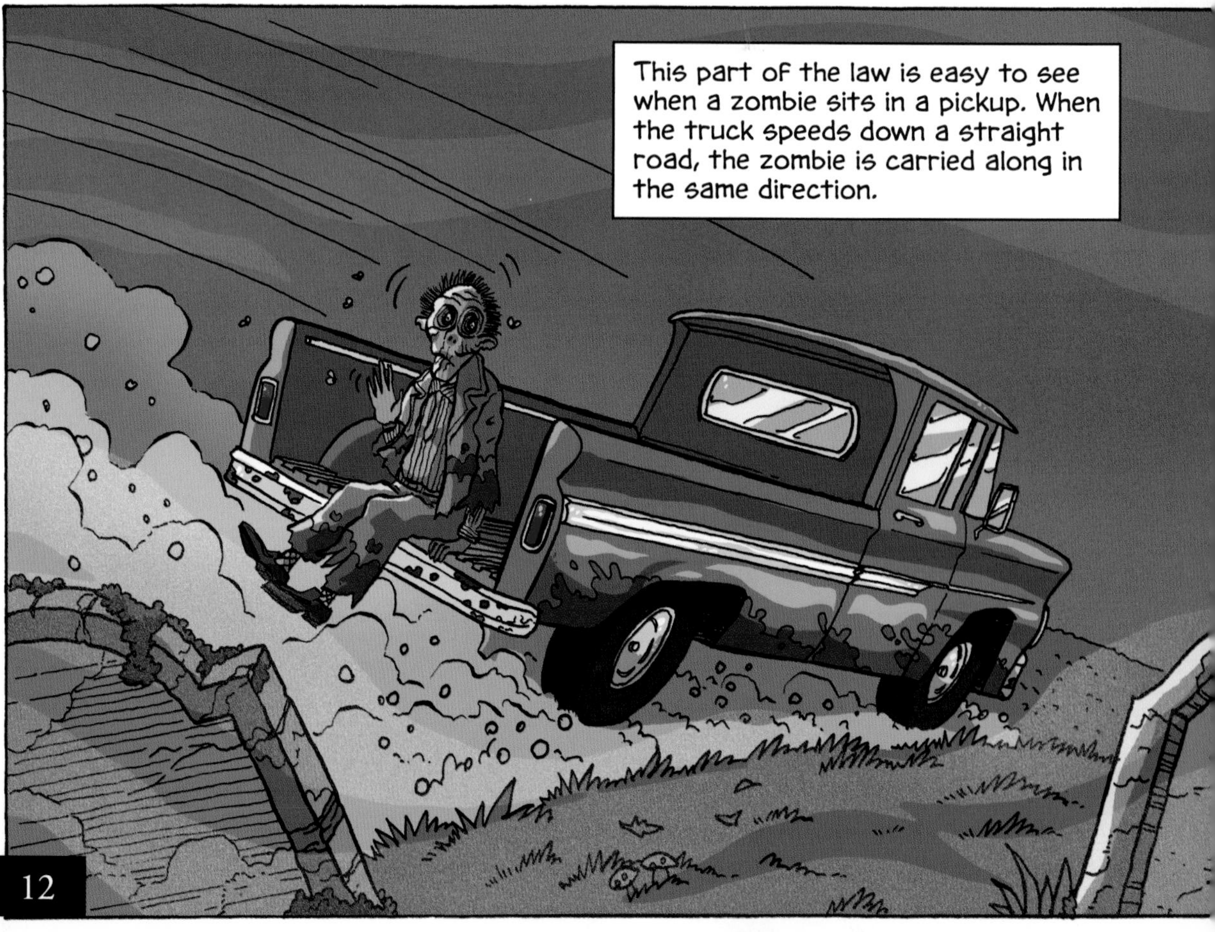
This part of the law is easy to see when a zombie sits in a pickup. When the truck speeds down a straight road, the zombie is carried along in the same direction.

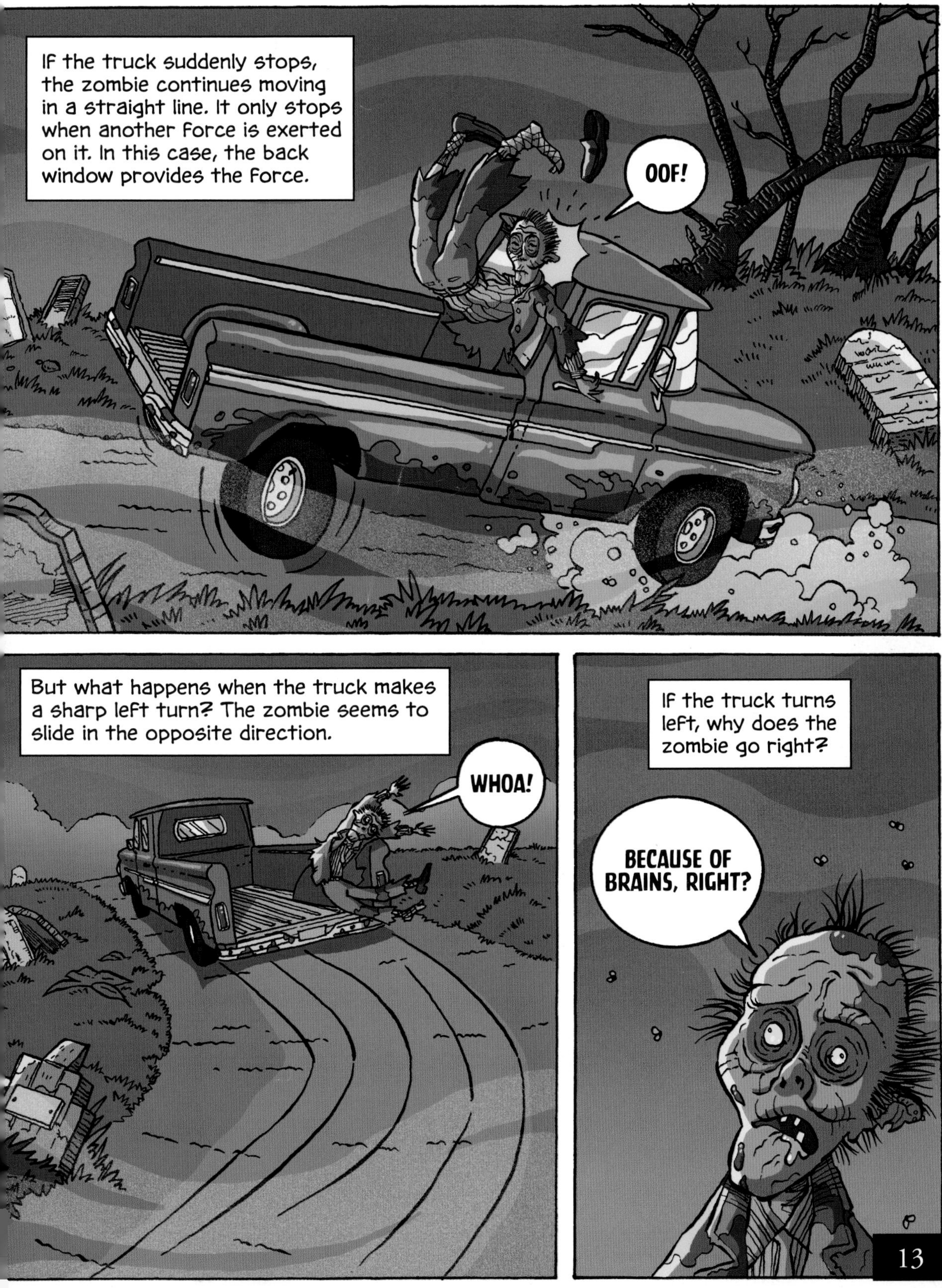
If the truck suddenly stops, the zombie continues moving in a straight line. It only stops when another force is exerted on it. In this case, the back window provides the force.
OOF!
But what happens when the truck makes a sharp left turn? The zombie seems to slide in the opposite direction.
WHOA!
If the truck turns left, why does the zombie go right?
BECAUSE OF BRAINS, RIGHT?

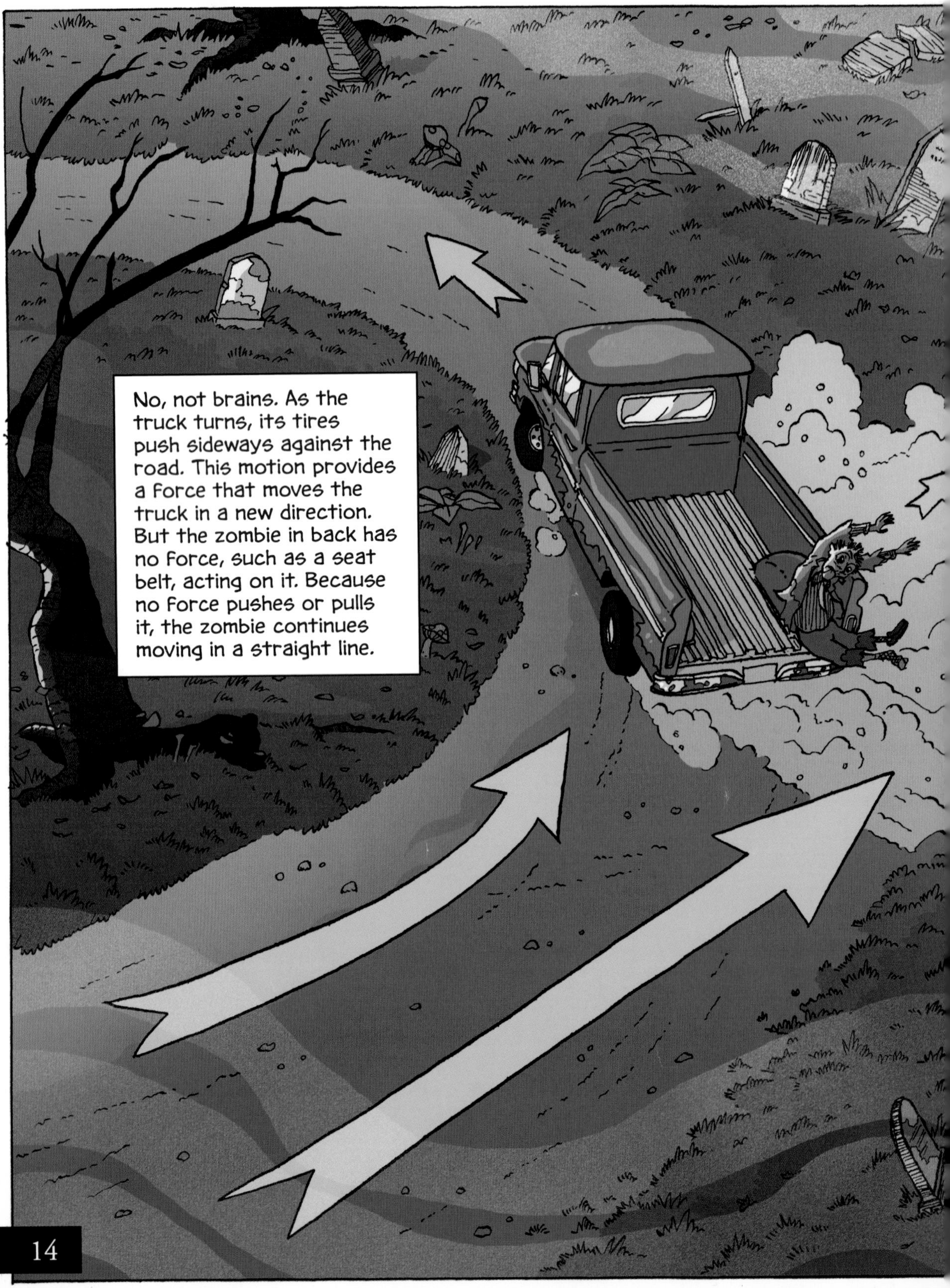
No, not brains. As the truck turns, its tires push sideways against the road. This motion provides a force that moves the truck in a new direction. But the zombie in back has no force, such as a seat belt, acting on it. Because no force pushes or pulls it, the zombie continues moving in a straight line.

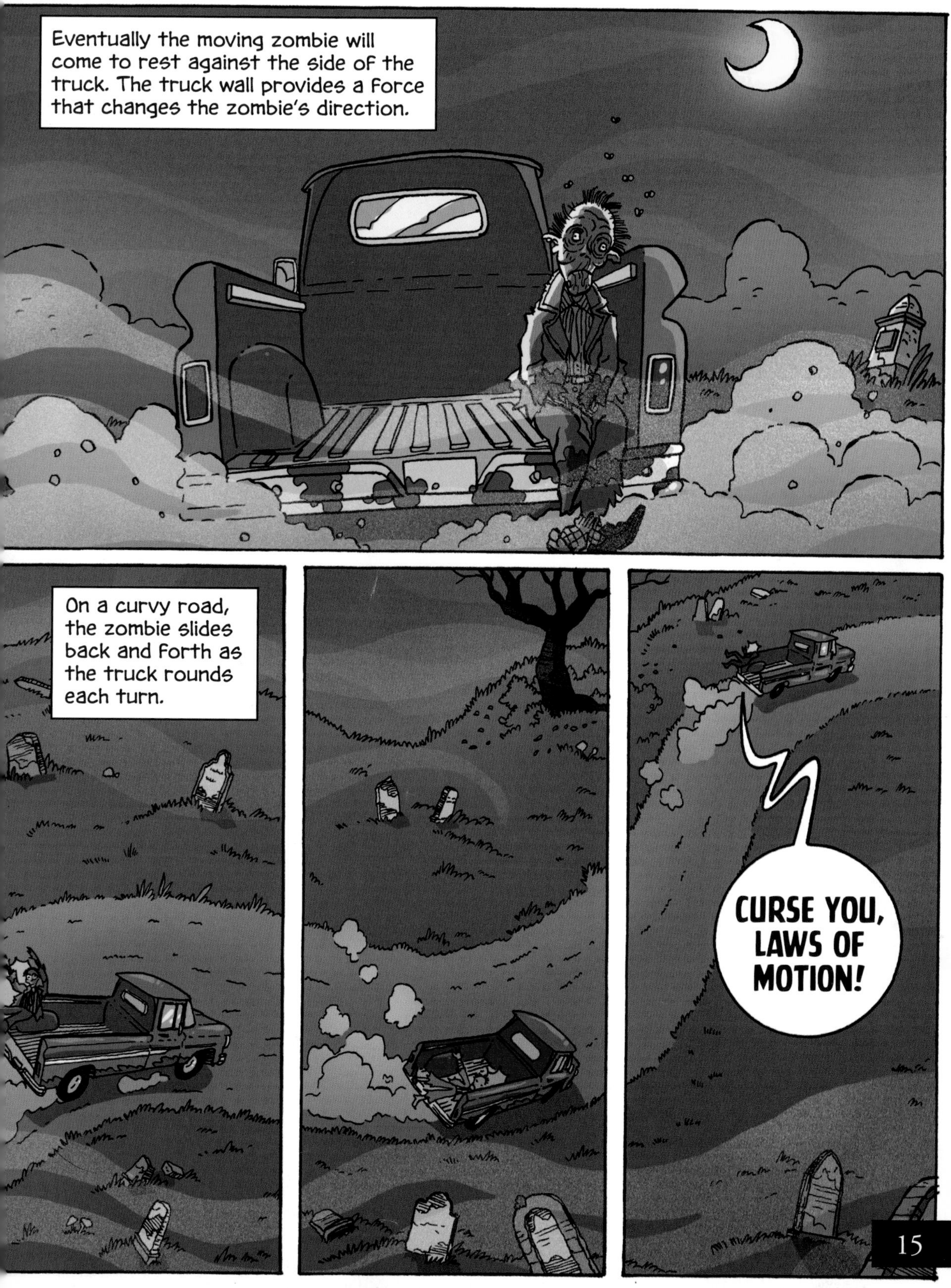
Eventually the moving zombie will come to rest against the side of the truck. The truck wall provides a force that changes the zombie's direction.
On a curvy road, the zombie slides back and forth as the truck rounds each turn.
CURSE YOU, LAWS OF MOTION!

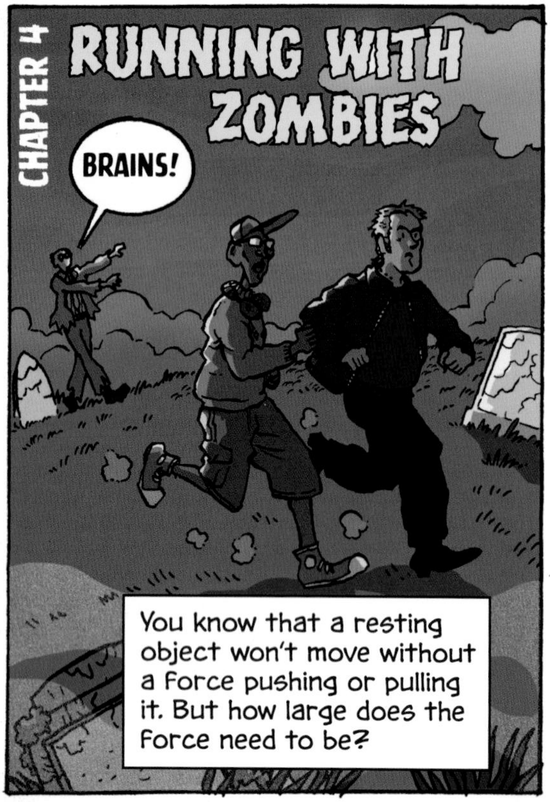
CHAPTER 4
RUNNING WITH ZOMBIES
BRAINS!
You know that a resting object won't move without a force pushing or pulling it. But how large does the force need to be?

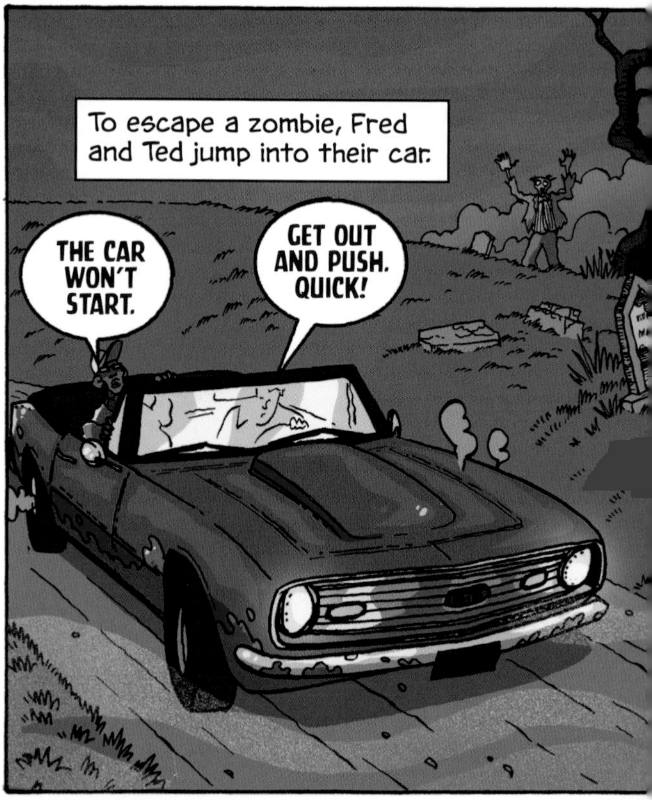
To escape a zombie, Fred and Ted jump into their car.
THE CAR WON'T START.
GET OUT AND PUSH. QUICK!

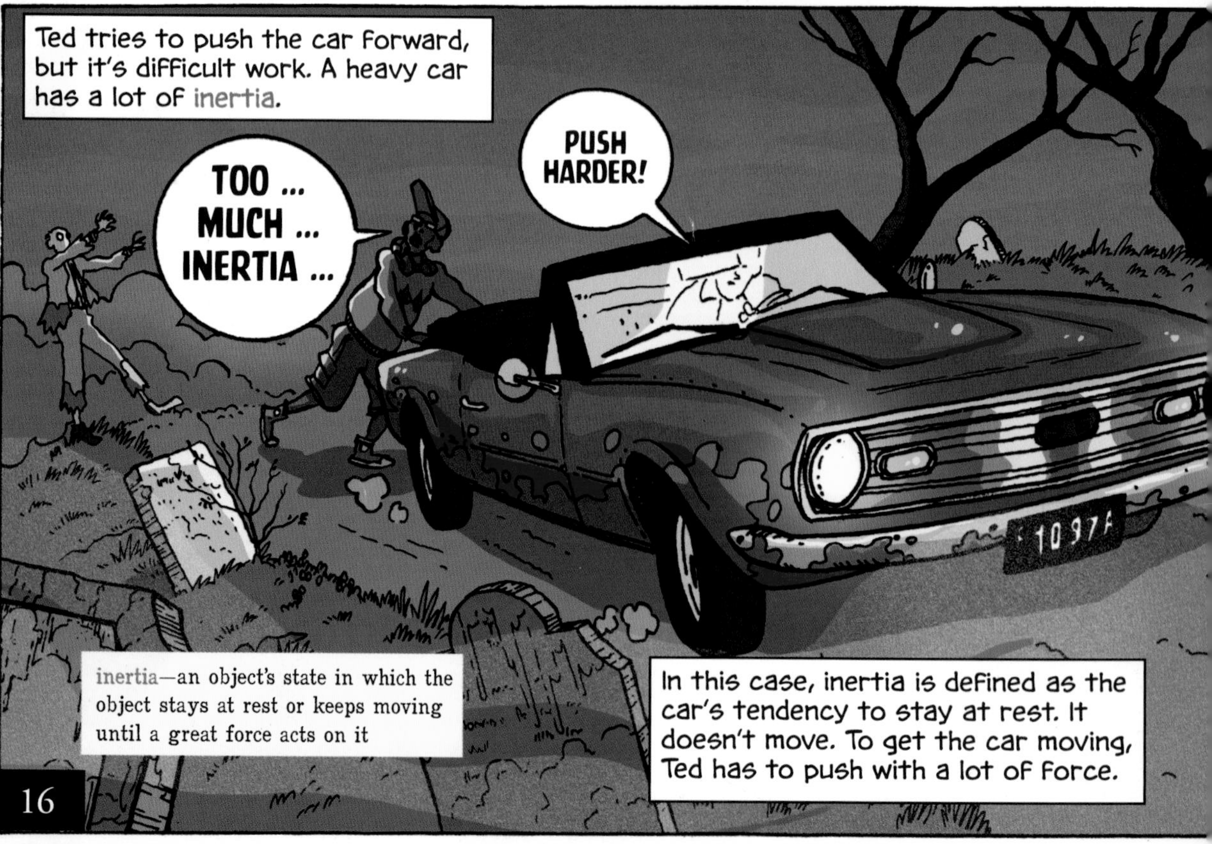
Ted tries to push the car forward, but it's difficult work. A heavy car has a lot of inertia.
TOO ... MUCH ... INERTIA ...
PUSH HARDER!
1097A
In this case, inertia is defined as the car's tendency to stay at rest. It doesn't move. To get the car moving, Ted has to push with a lot of force.

inertia—an object's state in which the object stays at rest or keeps moving until a great force acts on it

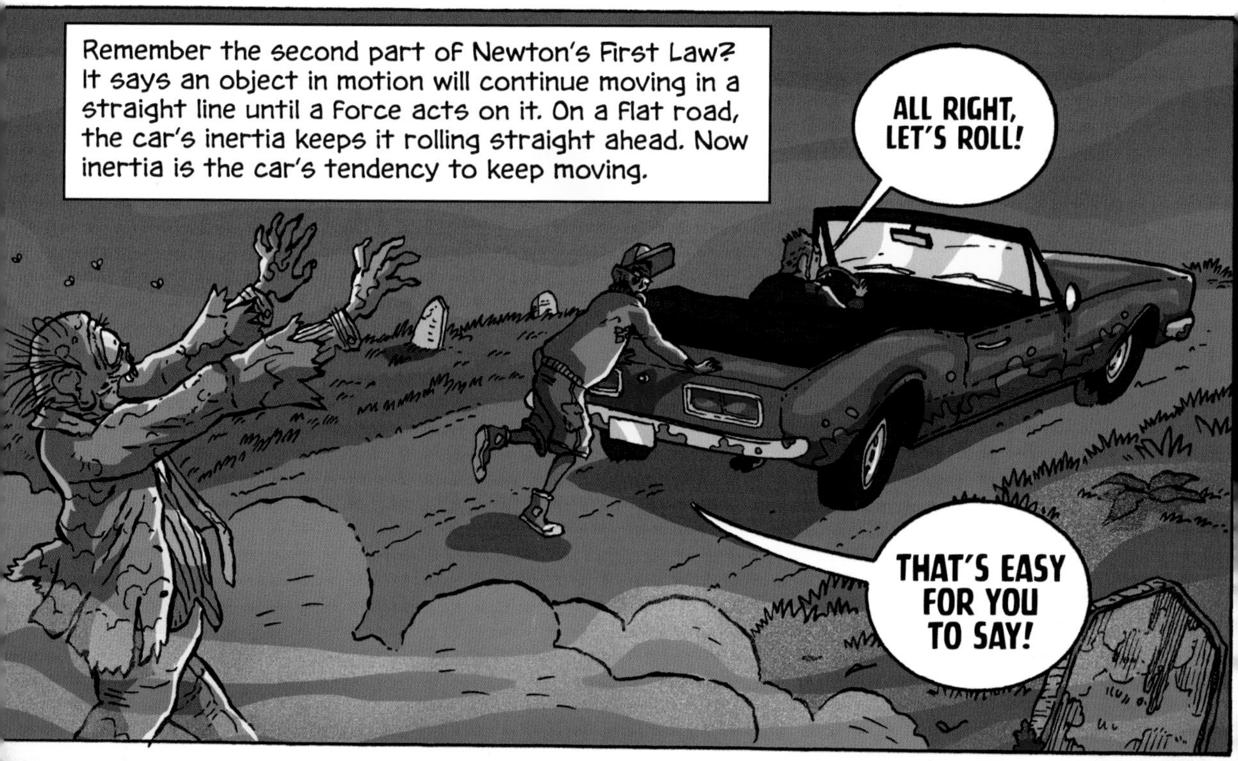
Remember the second part of Newton's First Law? It says an object in motion will continue moving in a straight line until a force acts on it. On a flat road, the car's inertia keeps it rolling straight ahead. Now inertia is the car's tendency to keep moving.
ALL RIGHT, LET'S ROLL!
THAT'S EASY FOR YOU TO SAY!

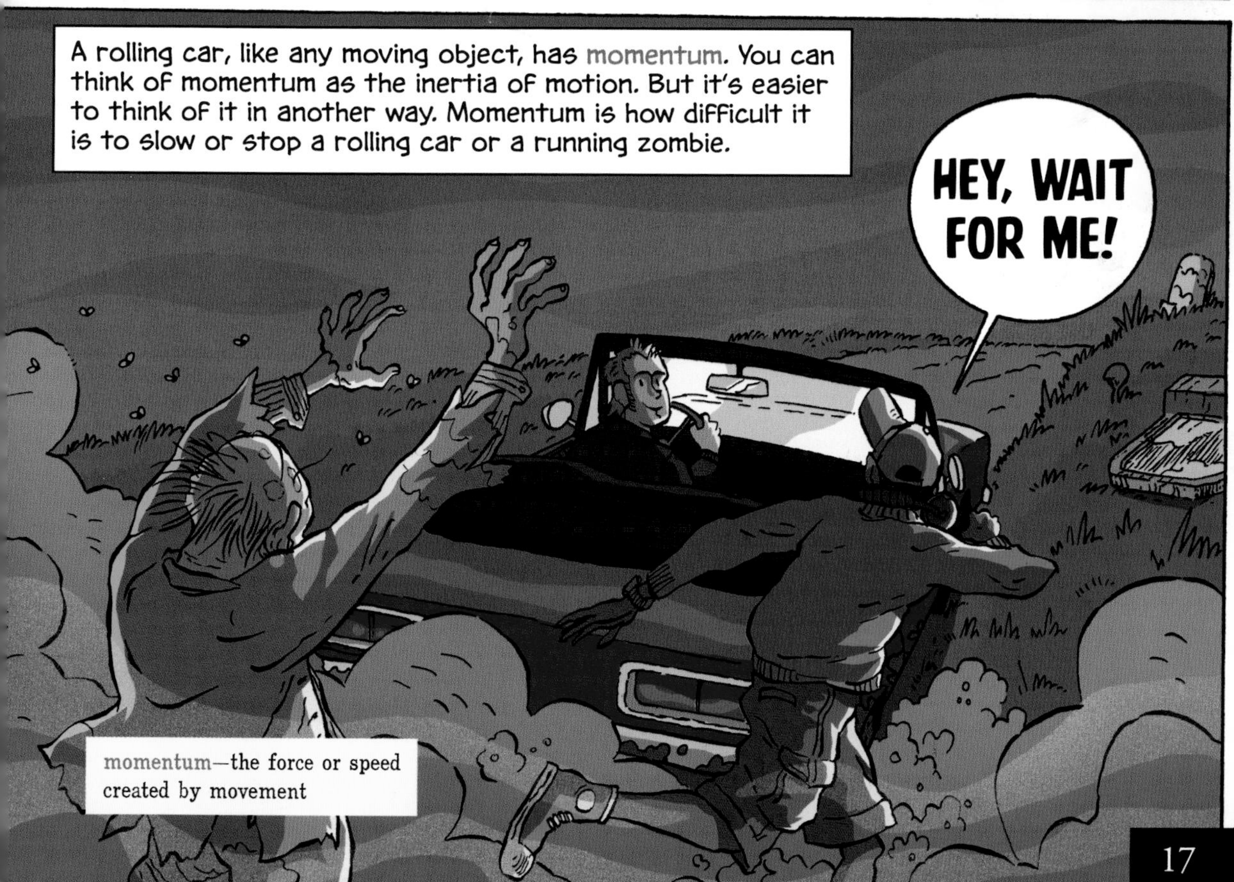
A rolling car, like any moving object, has momentum. You can think of momentum as the inertia of motion. But it's easier to think of it in another way. Momentum is how difficult it is to slow or stop a rolling car or a running zombie.
HEY, WAIT FOR ME!

momentum—the force or speed created by movement

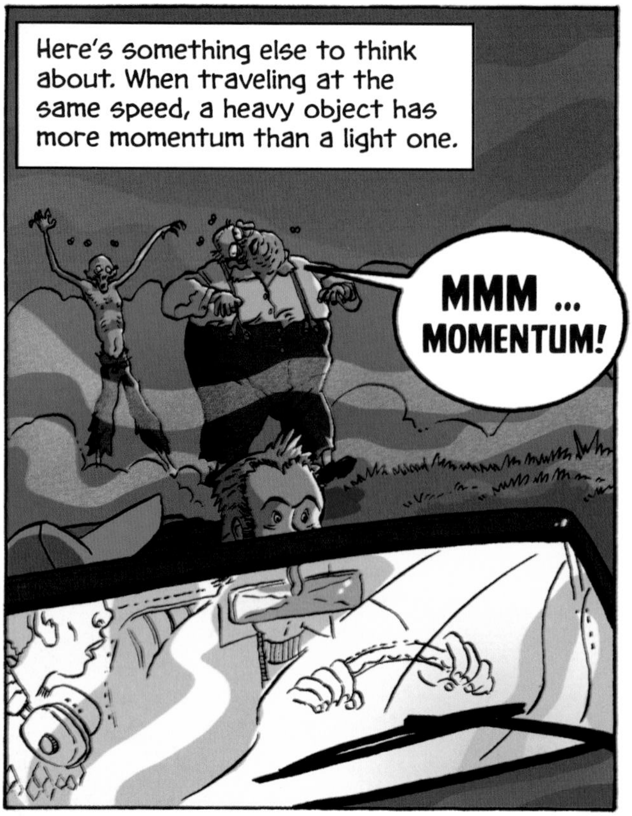
Here's something else to think about. When traveling at the same speed, a heavy object has more momentum than a light one.
MMM ... MOMENTUM!

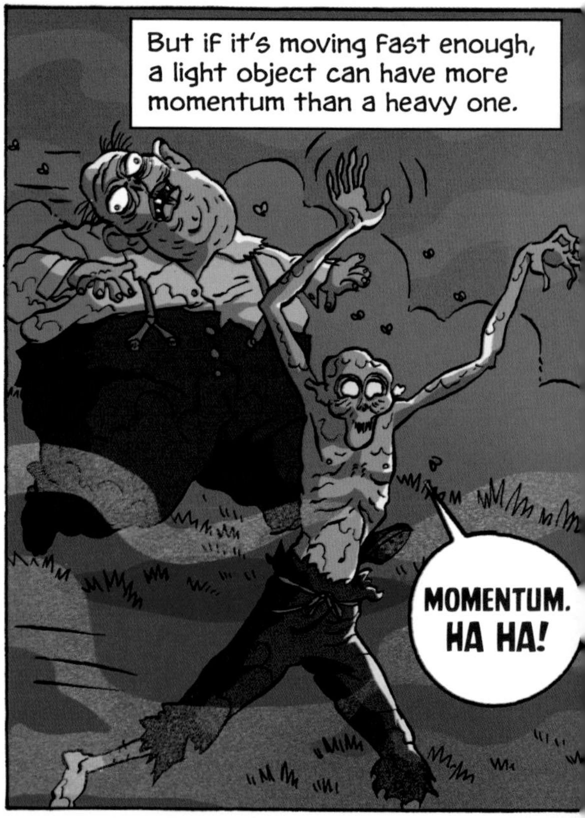
But if it's moving fast enough, a light object can have more momentum than a heavy one.
MOMENTUM. HA HA!

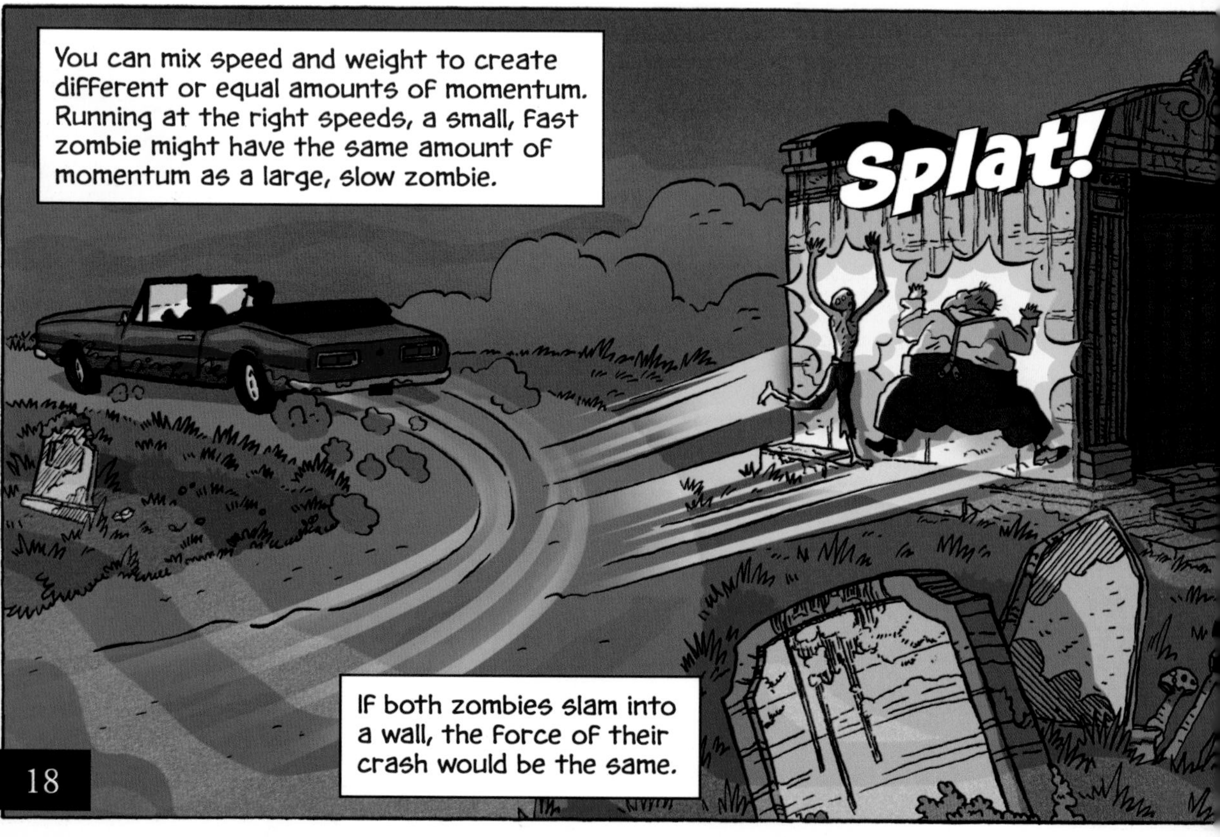
You can mix speed and weight to create different or equal amounts of momentum. Running at the right speeds, a small, fast zombie might have the same amount of momentum as a large, slow zombie.
Splat!
If both zombies slam into a wall, the force of their crash would be the same.

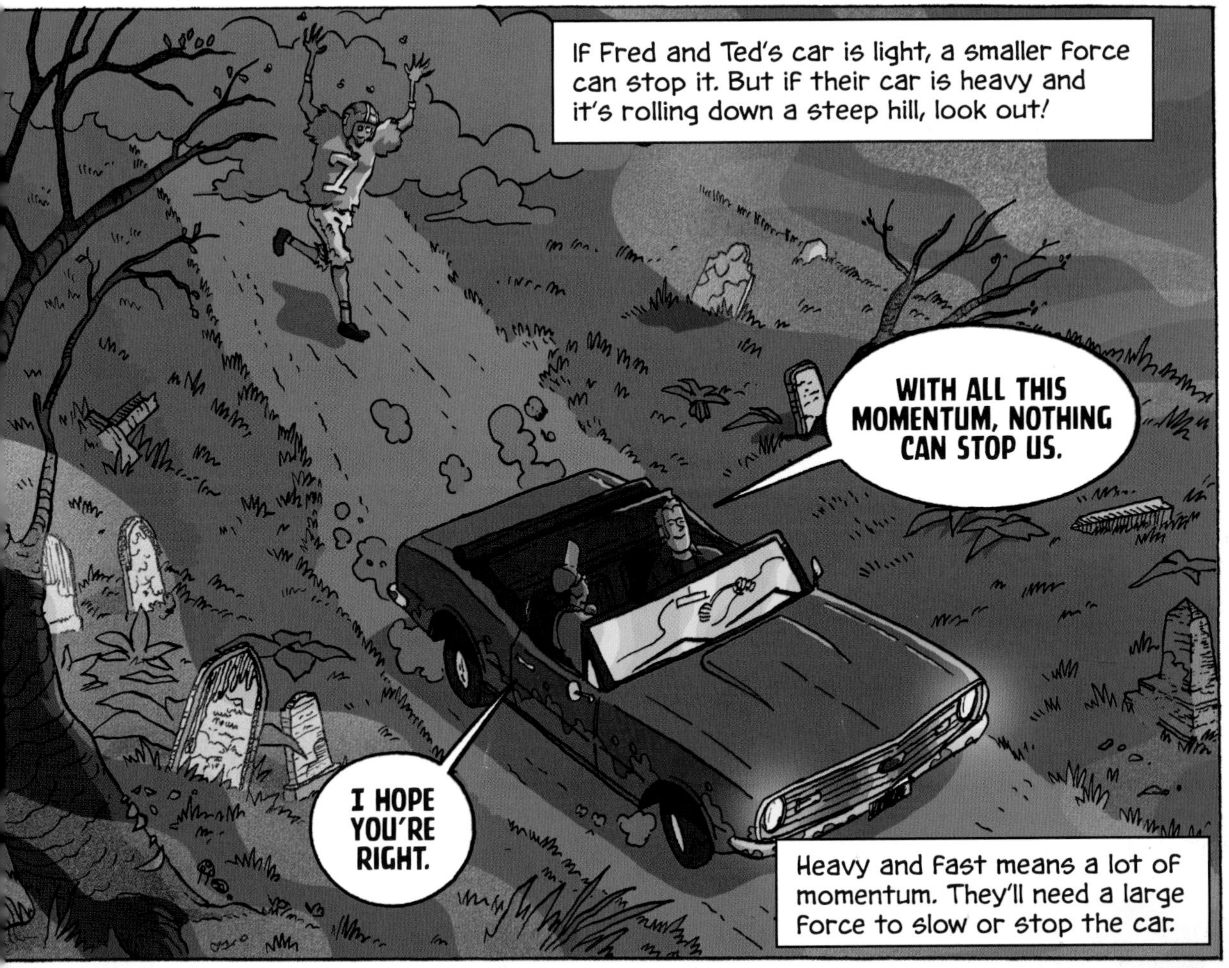
If Fred and Ted's car is light, a smaller force can stop it. But if their car is heavy and it's rolling down a steep hill, look out!
WITH ALL THIS MOMENTUM, NOTHING CAN STOP US.
I HOPE YOU'RE RIGHT.
Heavy and fast means a lot of momentum. They'll need a large force to slow or stop the car.

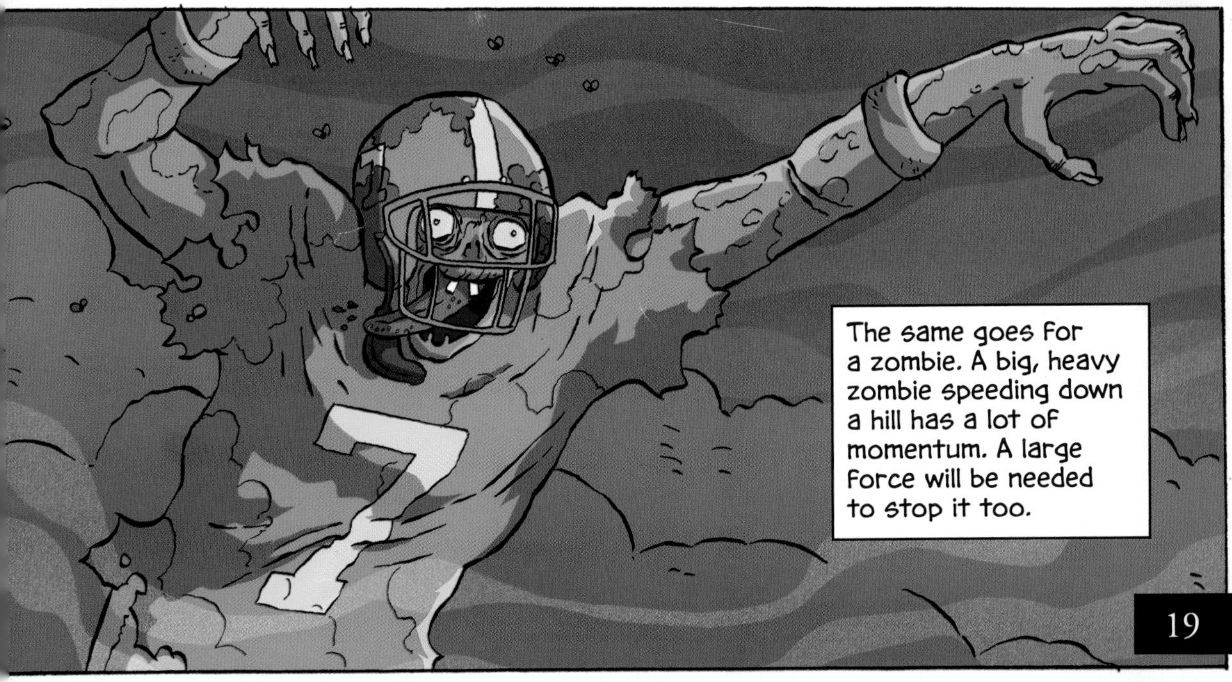
The same goes for a zombie. A big, heavy zombie speeding down a hill has a lot of momentum. A large force will be needed to stop it too.

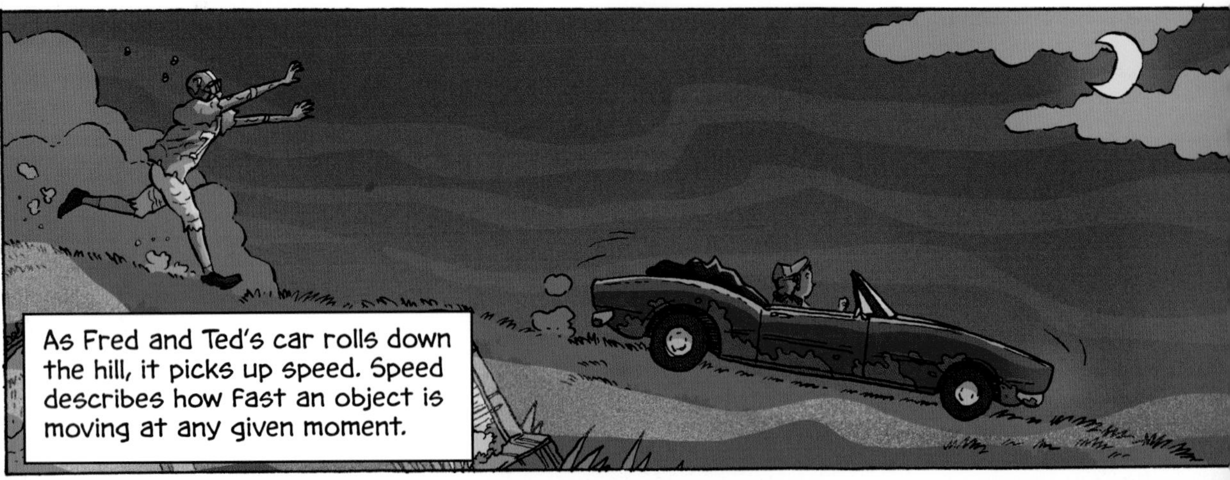
As Fred and Ted's car rolls down the hill, it picks up speed. Speed describes how fast an object is moving at any given moment.

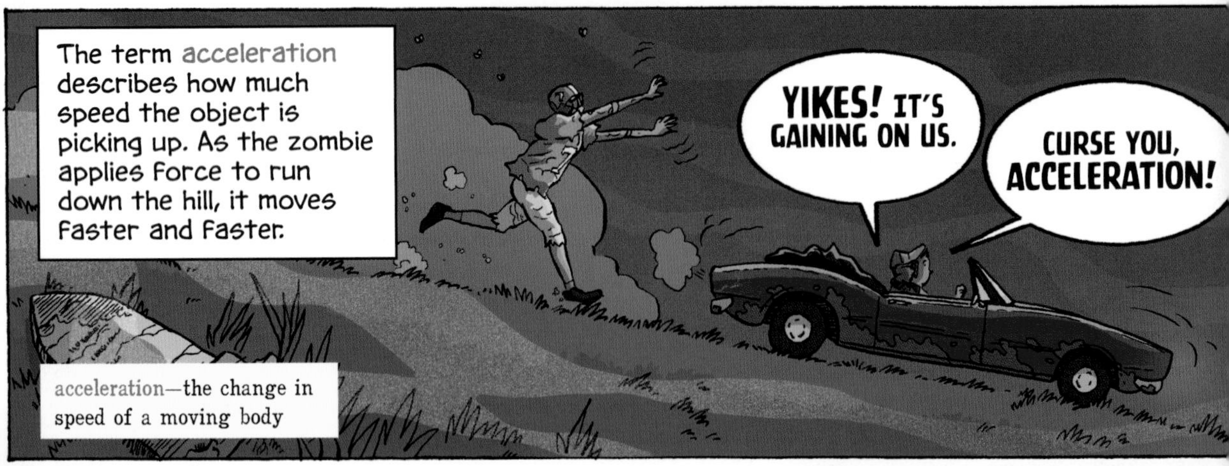
The term acceleration describes how much speed the object is picking up. As the zombie applies force to run down the hill, it moves faster and faster.
YIKES! IT'S GAINING ON US.
CURSE YOU, ACCELERATION!
acceleration—the change in speed of a moving body

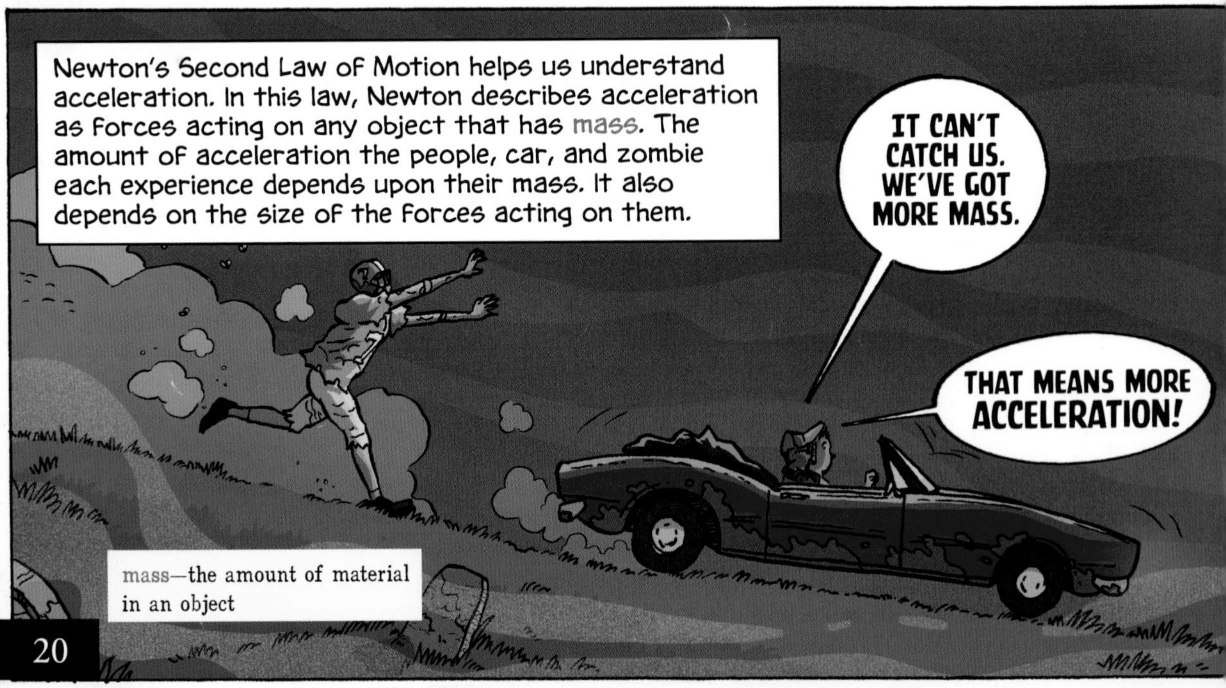
Newton's Second Law of Motion helps us understand acceleration. In this law, Newton describes acceleration as forces acting on any object that has mass. The amount of acceleration the people, car, and zombie each experience depends upon their mass. It also depends on the size of the forces acting on them.
IT CAN'T CATCH US. WE'VE GOT MORE MASS.
THAT MEANS MORE ACCELERATION!
mass—the amount of material in an object

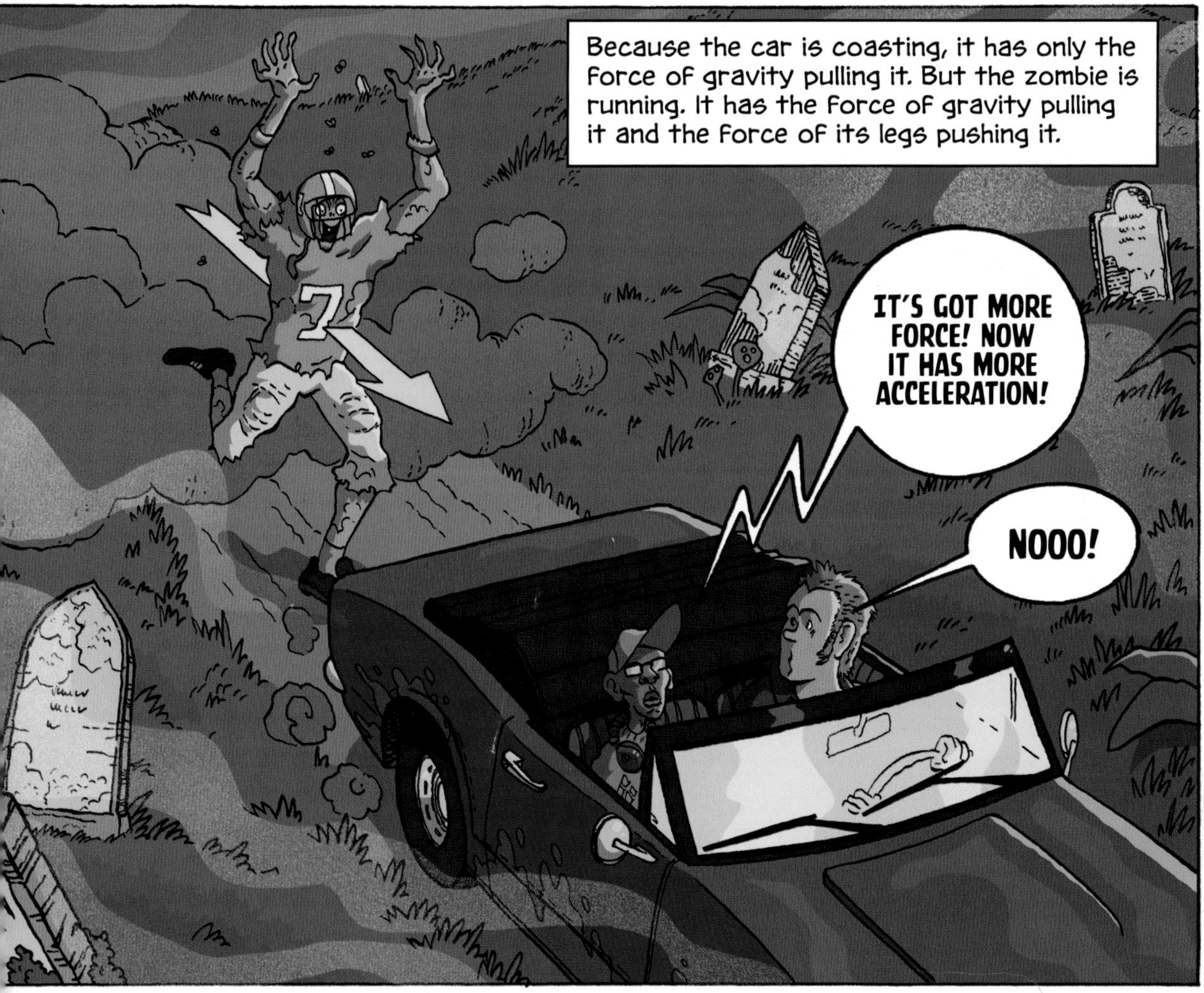
Because the car is coasting, it has only the force of gravity pulling it. But the zombie is running. It has the force of gravity pulling it and the force of its legs pushing it.
IT'S GOT MORE FORCE! NOW IT HAS MORE ACCELERATION!
NOOO!

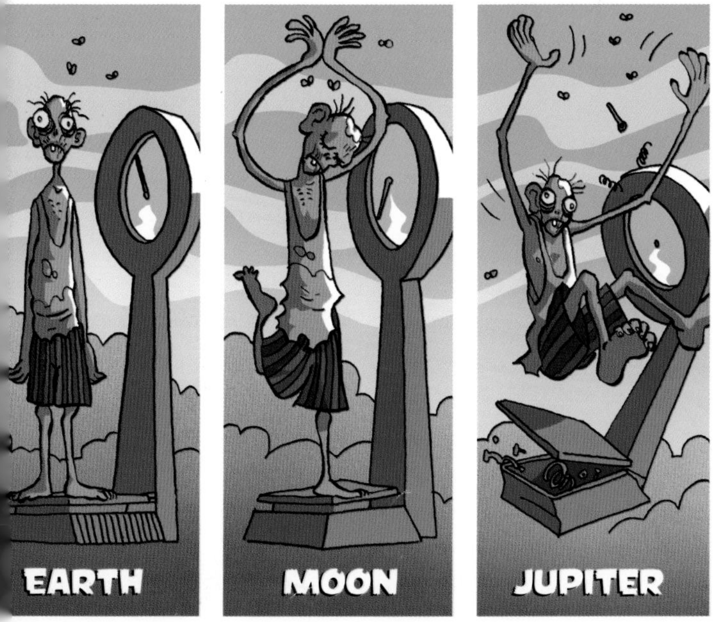
EARTH
MOON
JUPITER

MASS VS. WEIGHT

Mass describes the amount of matter in an object. An object's mass stays the same no matter where the object is. A zombie's mass measured on Earth, the moon, and Jupiter is the same.

But weight depends on gravity. The force of gravity is different on Earth, the moon, and Jupiter. A zombie on Earth might weighs 200 pounds (91 kilograms). On the moon he would weigh only 33 pounds (15 kg). On Jupiter he would weigh a whopping 473 pounds (215 kg)!

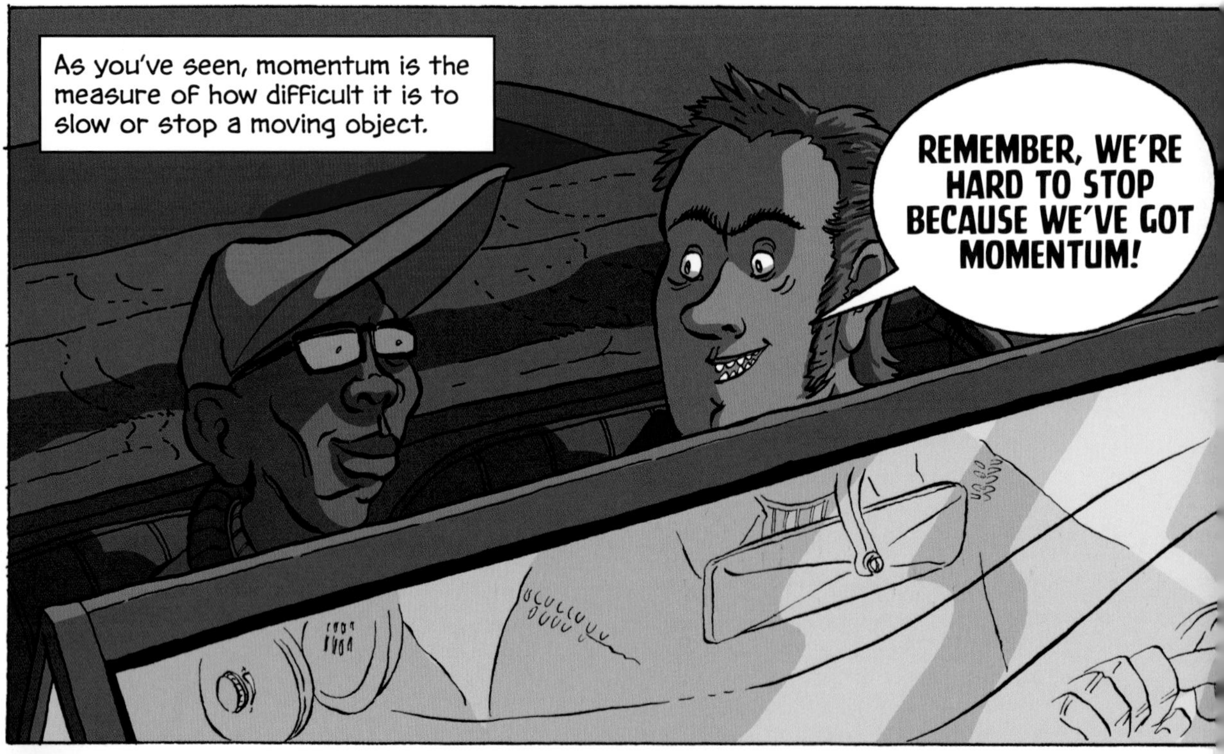
As you've seen, momentum is the measure of how difficult it is to slow or stop a moving object.
REMEMBER, WE'RE HARD TO STOP BECAUSE WE'VE GOT MOMENTUM!

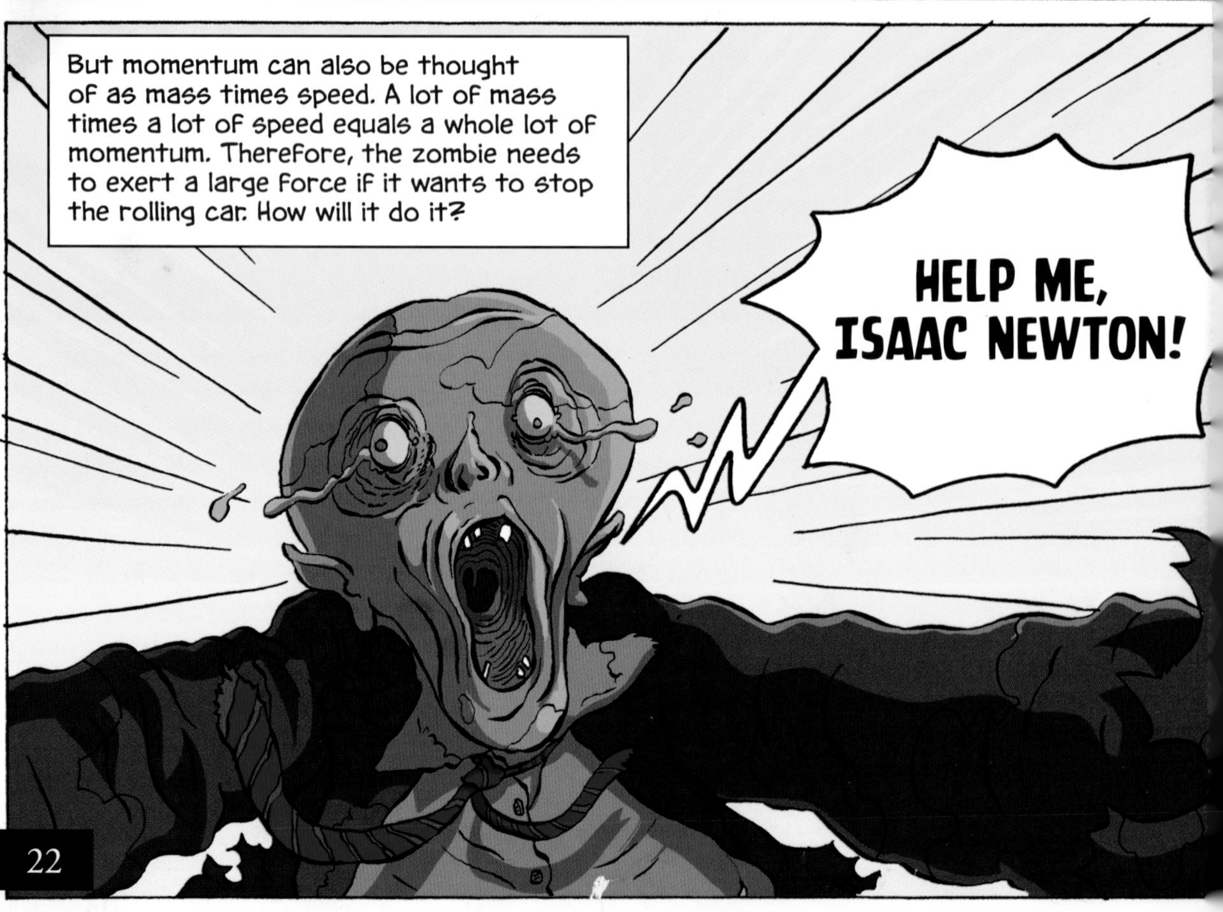
But momentum can also be thought of as mass times speed. A lot of mass times a lot of speed equals a whole lot of momentum. Therefore, the zombie needs to exert a large force if it wants to stop the rolling car. How will it do it?
HELP ME, ISAAC NEWTON!

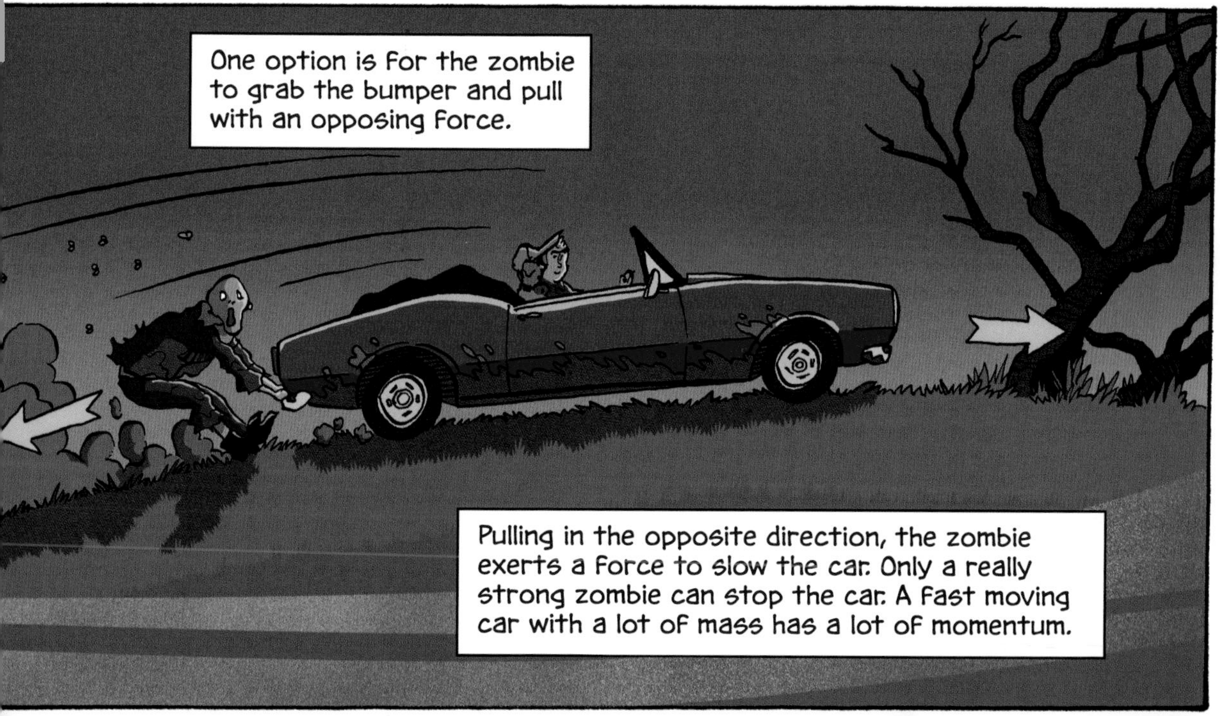
One option is for the zombie to grab the bumper and pull with an opposing force.
Pulling in the opposite direction, the zombie exerts a force to slow the car. Only a really strong zombie can stop the car. A fast moving car with a lot of mass has a lot of momentum.

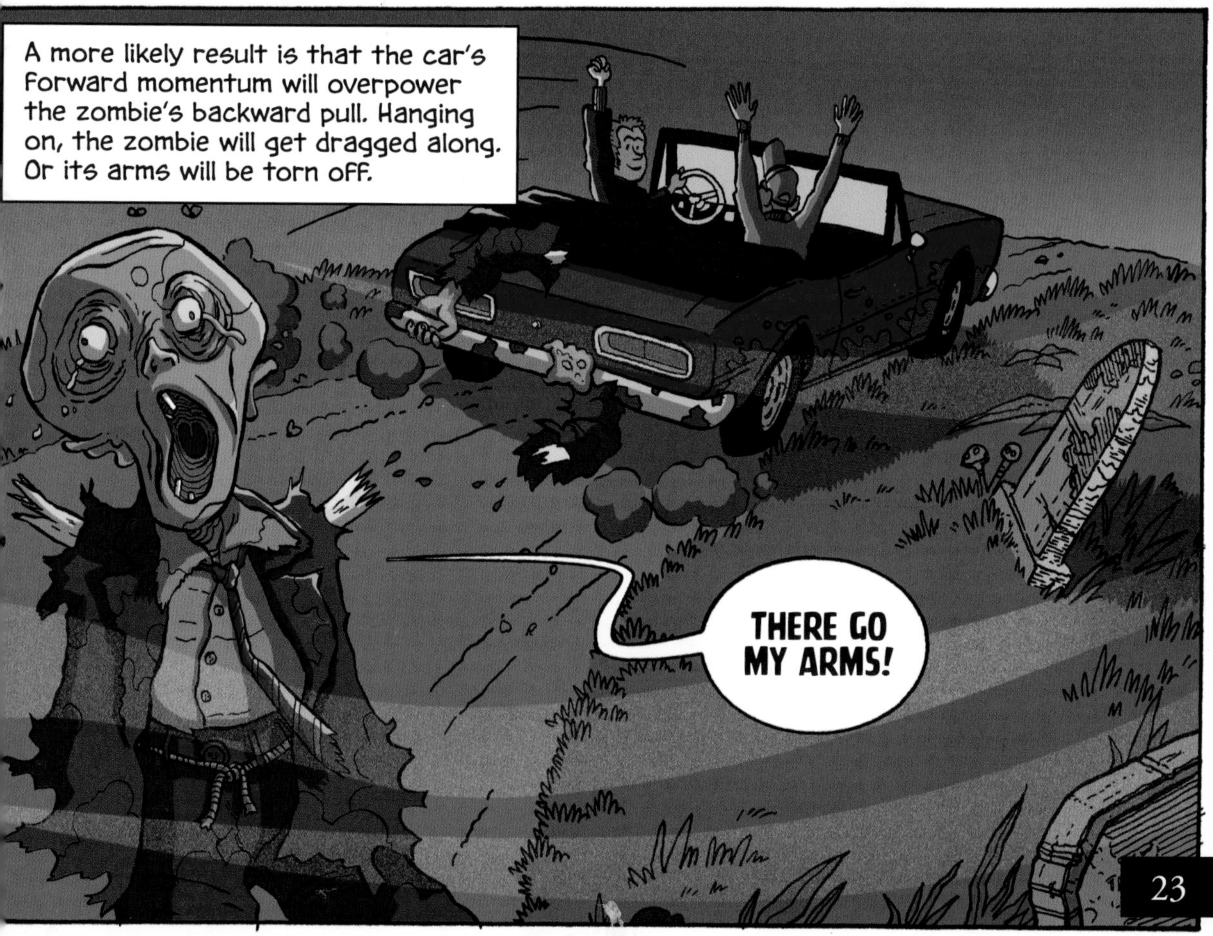
A more likely result is that the car's forward momentum will overpower the zombie's backward pull. Hanging on, the zombie will get dragged along. Or its arms will be torn off.
THERE GO MY ARMS!

Chapter 5 Fleshing Out Friction

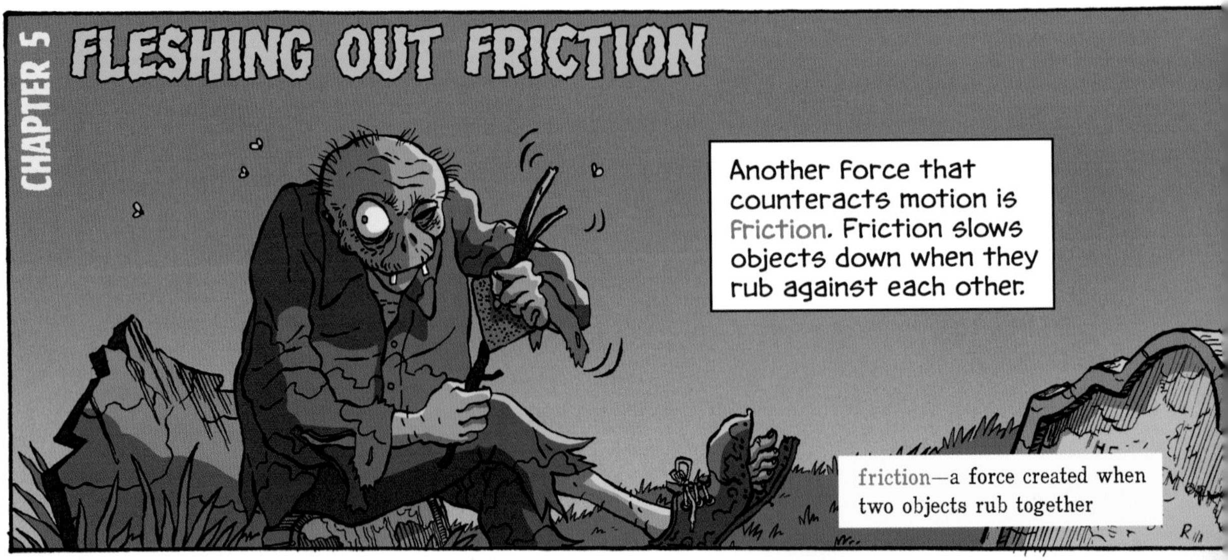
Another force that counteracts motion is friction. Friction slows objects down when they rub against each other.

friction—a force created when two objects rub together

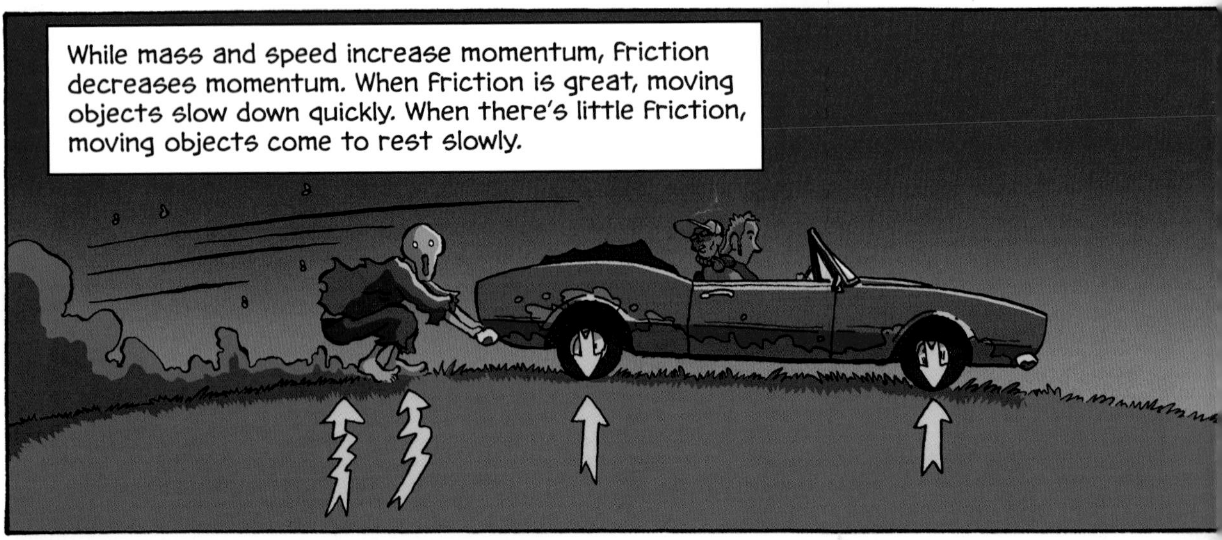
While mass and speed increase momentum, friction decreases momentum. When friction is great, moving objects slow down quickly. When there's little friction, moving objects come to rest slowly.

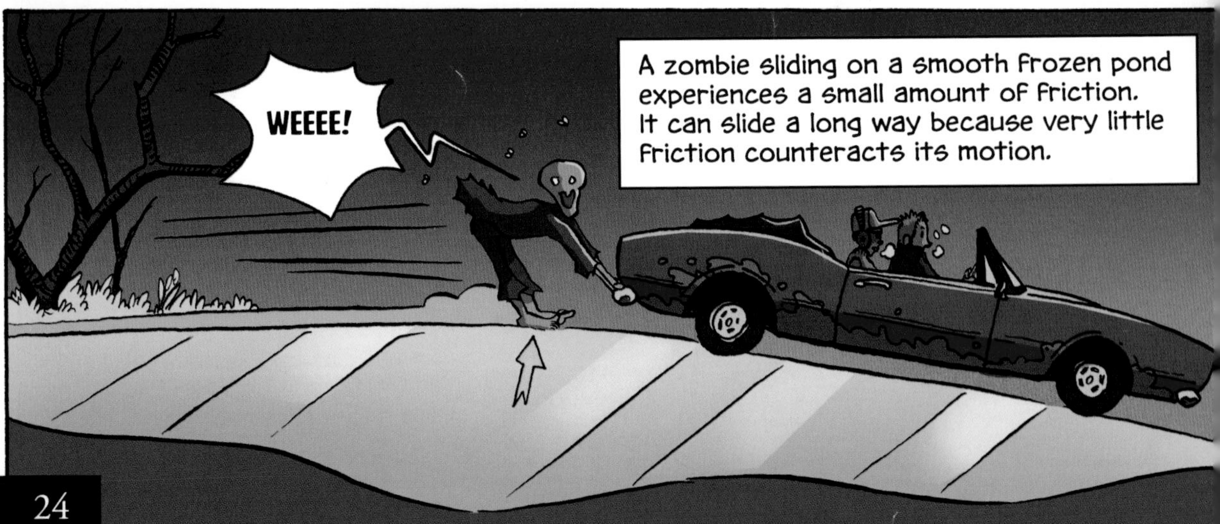
WEEEE!
A zombie sliding on a smooth frozen pond experiences a small amount of friction. It can slide a long way because very little friction counteracts its motion.

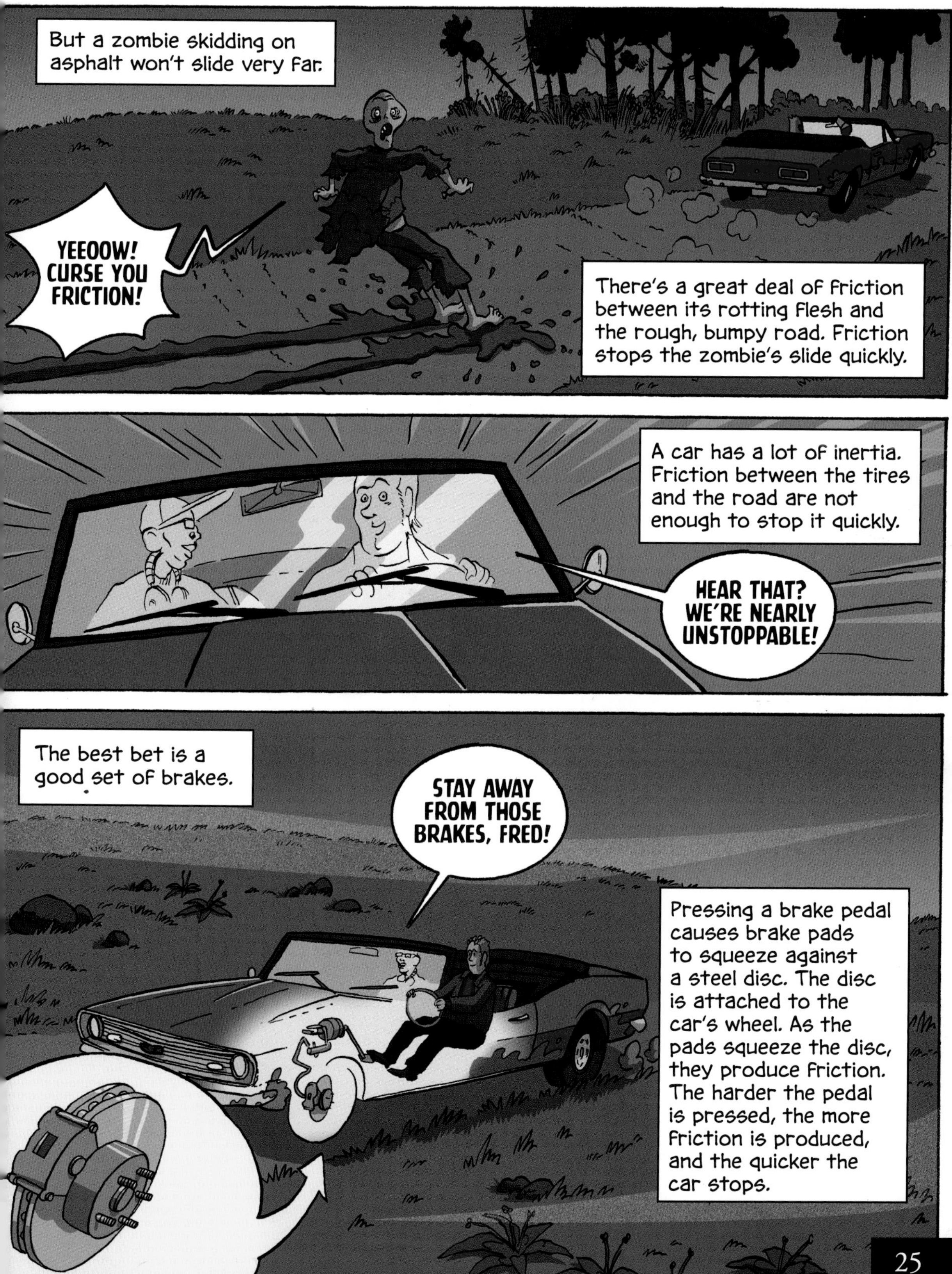
But a zombie skidding on asphalt won't slide very far.
YEEOOW! CURSE YOU FRICTION!
There's a great deal of friction between its rotting flesh and the rough, bumpy road. Friction stops the zombie's slide quickly.
A car has a lot of inertia. Friction between the tires and the road are not enough to stop it quickly.
HEAR THAT? WE'RE NEARLY UNSTOPPABLE!
The best bet is a good set of brakes.
STAY AWAY FROM THOSE BRAKES, FRED!
Pressing a brake pedal causes brake pads to squeeze against a steel disc. The disc is attached to the car's wheel. As the pads squeeze the disc, they produce friction. The harder the pedal is pressed, the more friction is produced, and the quicker the car stops.

CHAPTER 6 ZOMBIE ACTION AND REACTION

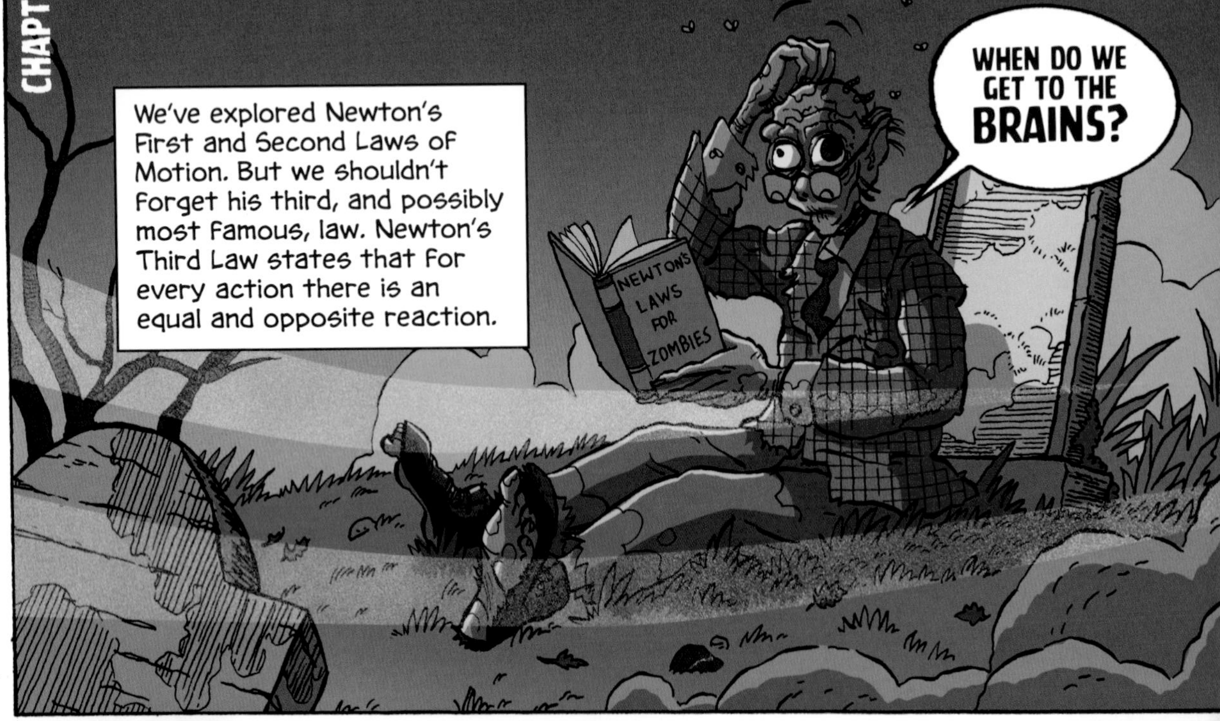
We've explored Newton's First and Second Laws of Motion. But we shouldn't forget his third, and possibly most famous, law. Newton's Third Law states that for every action there is an equal and opposite reaction.
WHEN DO WE GET TO THE BRAINS?
NEWTON'S LAWS FOR ZOMBIES

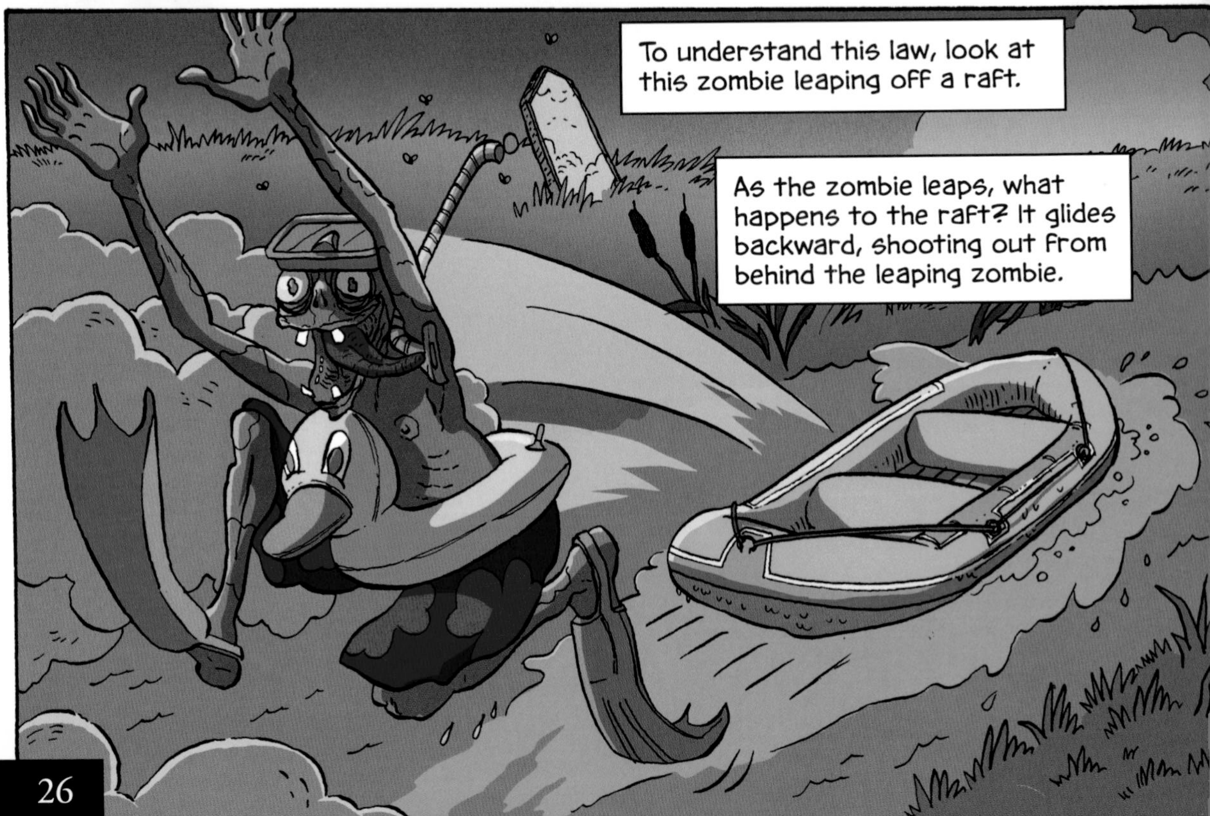
To understand this law, look at this zombie leaping off a raft.
As the zombie leaps, what happens to the raft? It glides backward, shooting out from behind the leaping zombie.

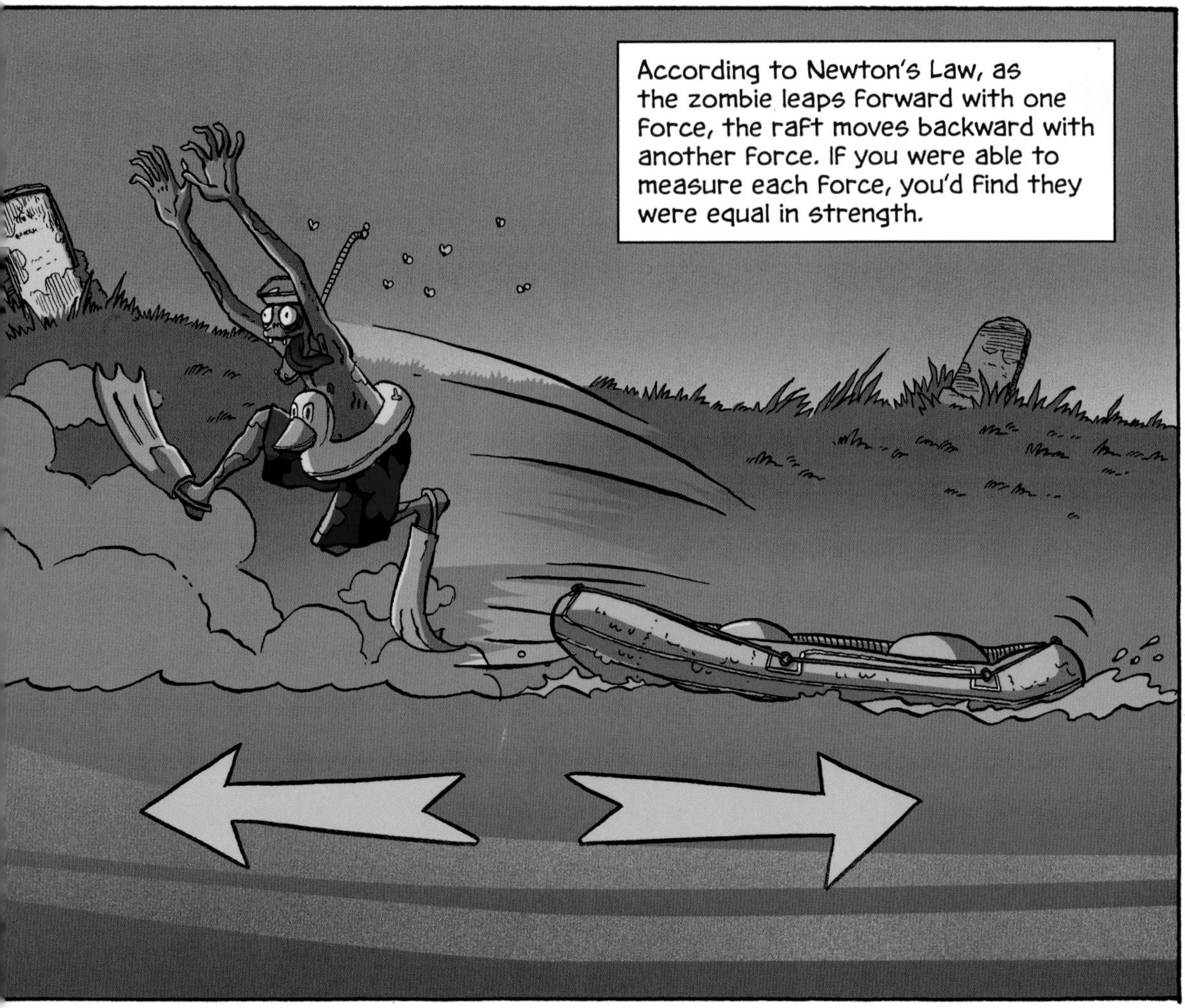
According to Newton's Law, as the zombie leaps forward with one force, the raft moves backward with another force. If you were able to measure each force, you'd find they were equal in strength.

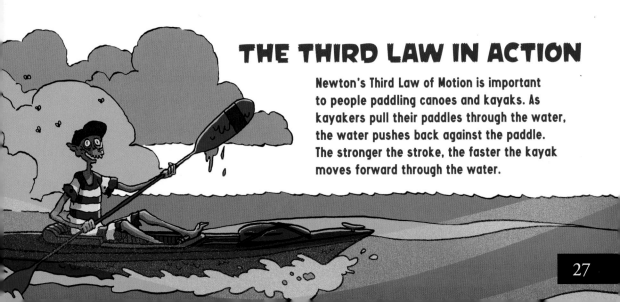

THE THIRD LAW IN ACTION

Newton's Third Law of Motion is important to people paddling canoes and kayaks. As kayakers pull their paddles through the water, the water pushes back against the paddle. The stronger the stroke, the faster the kayak moves forward through the water.

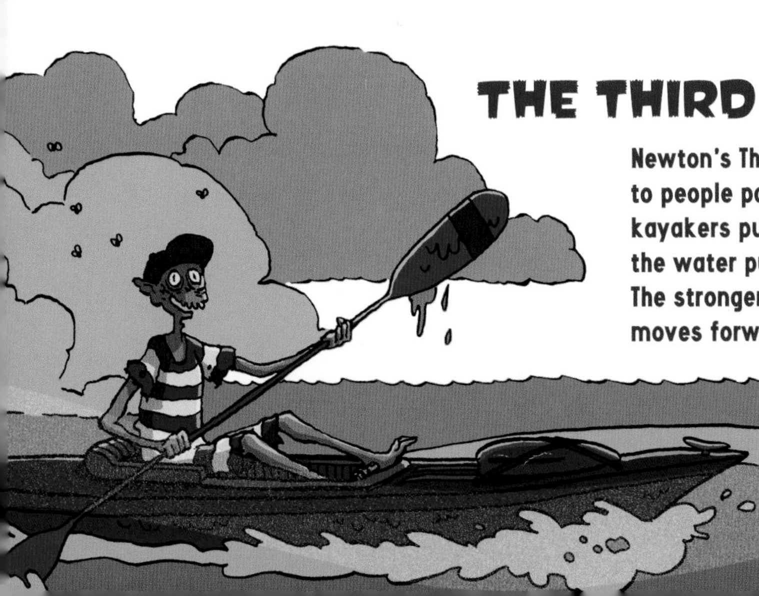

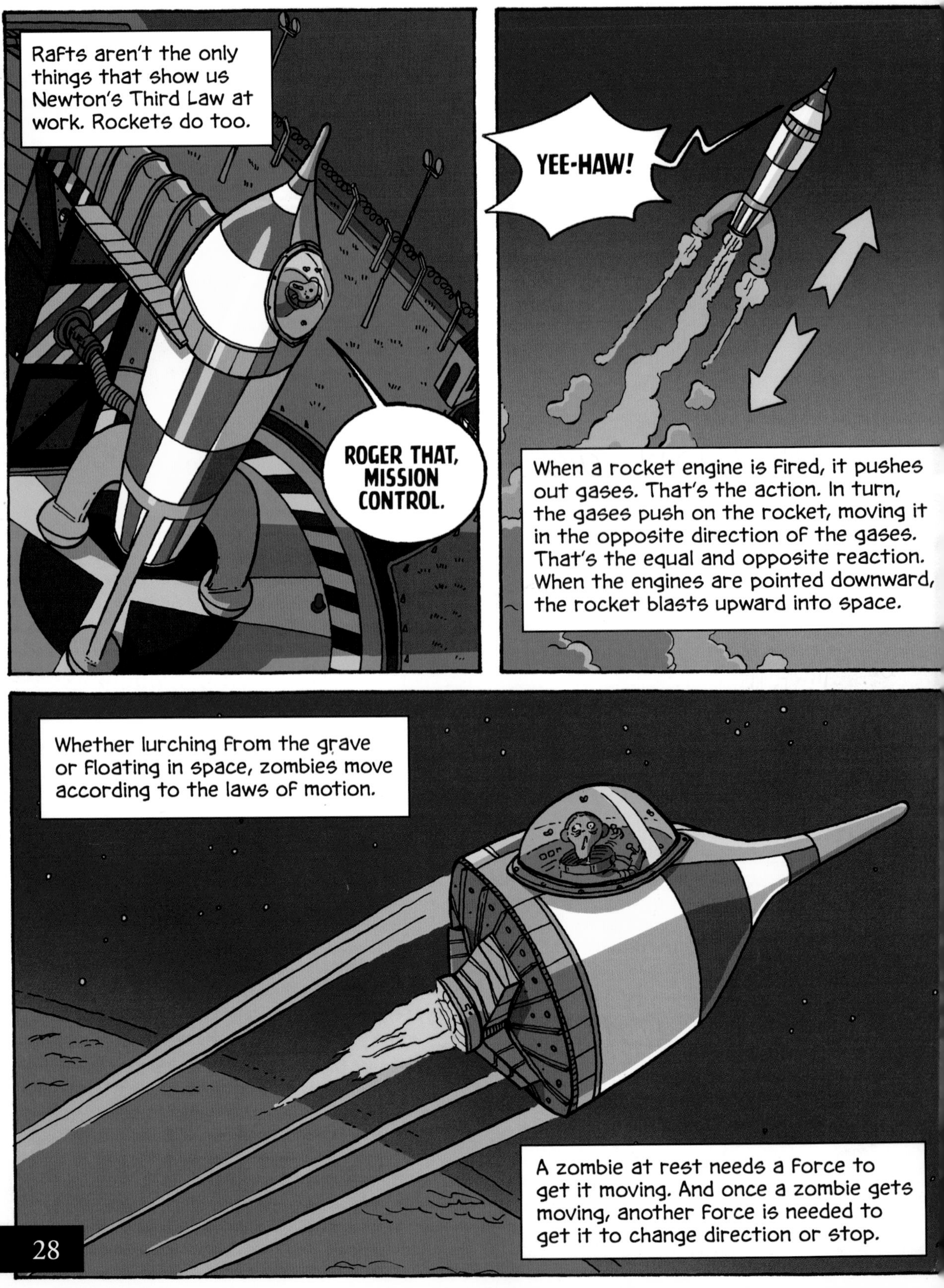
Rafts aren't the only things that show us Newton's Third Law at work. Rockets do too.
ROGER THAT, MISSION CONTROL.
YEE-HAW!
When a rocket engine is fired, it pushes out gases. That's the action. In turn, the gases push on the rocket, moving it in the opposite direction of the gases. That's the equal and opposite reaction. When the engines are pointed downward, the rocket blasts upward into space.
Whether lurching from the grave or floating in space, zombies move according to the laws of motion.
A zombie at rest needs a force to get it moving. And once a zombie gets moving, another force is needed to get it to change direction or stop.

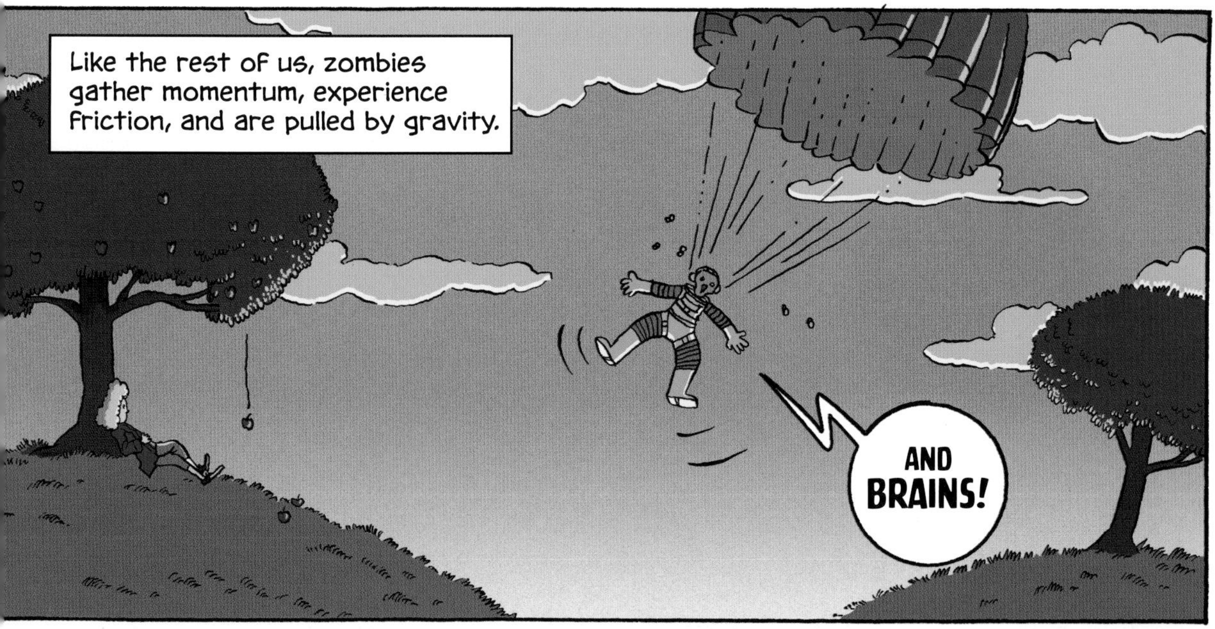
Like the rest of us, zombies gather momentum, experience friction, and are pulled by gravity.
AND BRAINS!

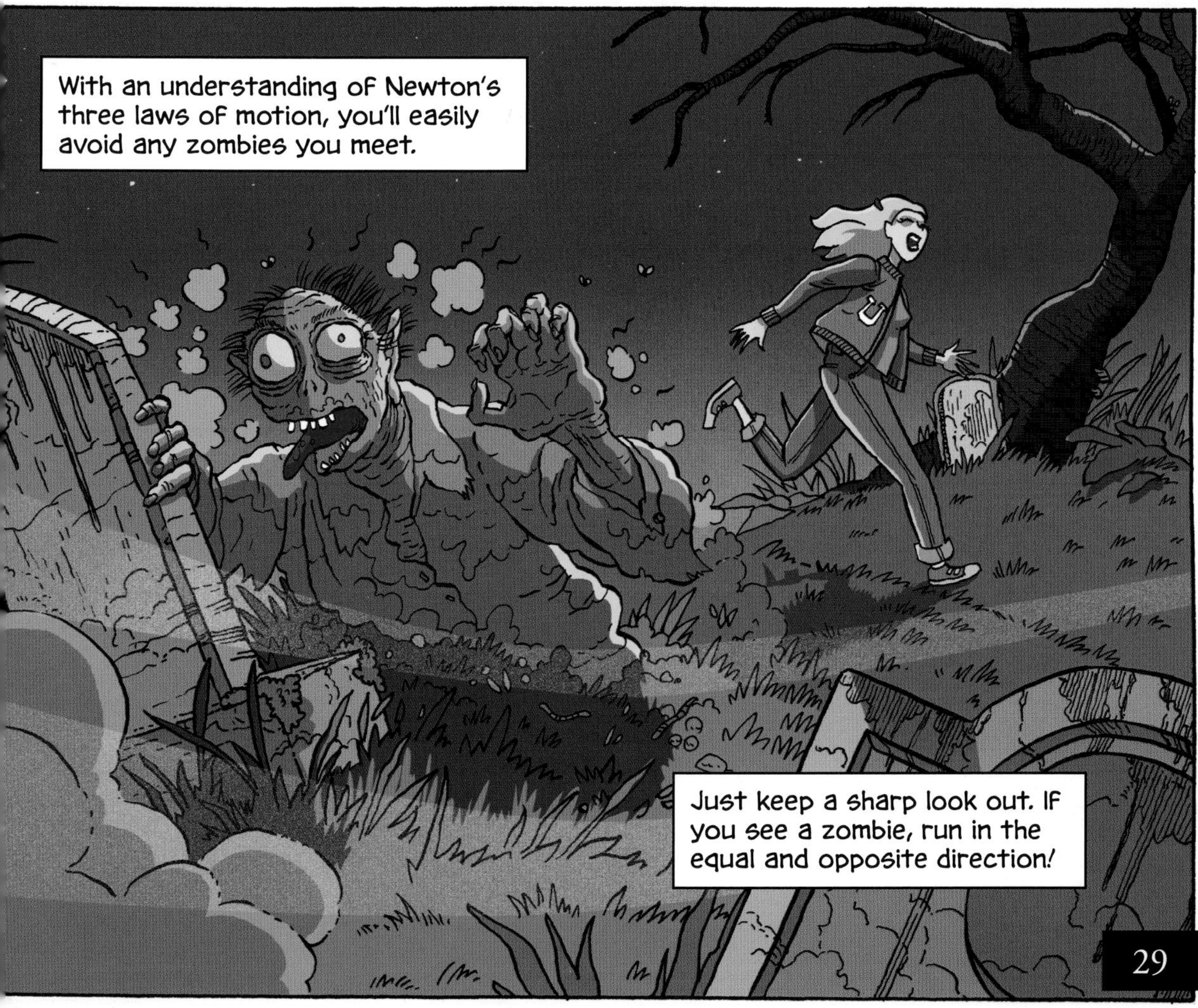
With an understanding of Newton's three laws of motion, you'll easily avoid any zombies you meet.
Just keep a sharp look out. If you see a zombie, run in the equal and opposite direction!

GLOSSARY

acceleration (ak-sel-uh-RAY-shuhn)—the change in speed of a moving body

exert (eg-ZURT)—to make an effort to do something

force (FORS)—any action that changes the movement of an object

friction (FRIK-shuhn)—a force created when two objects rub together; friction slows down objects

gravity (GRAV-uh-tee)—a force that pulls objects with mass together; gravity pulls objects down toward the center of earth

inertia (in-UR-shuh)—an object's state in which the object stays at rest or keeps moving in the same direction until a greater force acts on the object

mass (MASS)—the amount of material in an object

matter (MAT-ur)—anything that has weight and takes up space

momentum (moh-MEN-tuhm)—the force or speed created by movement

pressure (PRESH-ur)—a force that pushes on something

prism (PRIZ-uhm)—a transparent, triangle-shaped plastic or glass object that bends light

READ MORE

Lepora, Nathan. *Twists and Turns: Forces in Motion.* The Science Behind Thrill Rides. Pleasantville, N.Y.: Gareth Stevens Pub., 2008.

Sohn, Emily. *A Crash Course in Forces and Motion with Max Axiom, Super Scientist.* Graphic Science. Mankato, Minn.: Capstone Press, 2007.

Whiting, Jim. *The Science of Hitting a Home Run: Forces and Motion in Action.* Action Science. Mankato, Minn.: Capstone Press, 2010.

INTERNET SITES

FactHound offers a safe, fun way to find Internet sites related to this book. All sites on FactHound have been researched by our staff.

Here's all you do:

Visit *www.facthound.com*

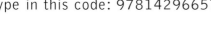

Type in this code: 9781429665773

Check out projects, games and lots more at
www.capstonekids.com

INDEX